WHILE WE ARE STILL SINNERS

The Road to Redemption Through Christ

DEDICATION

To the weary seekers, the silent sufferers,
to those who have wandered in shadows of loss,
who have carried shame, guilt, or the weight of unworthiness—
I see you.

This book was placed on my heart through the Holy Spirit for you,
that you might feel the embrace of the Holy Trinity
and hear the whisper of Jesus calling you home.
Right where you are, He loves you—
fully, endlessly, immeasurably.

THE JOURNEY

Your walk with God is the most pivotal and momentous journey you will ever take. The path is filled with dark valleys and beautiful views, each twist and turn revealing a new truth, testing your beliefs, and building your armor. It takes courage to turn away from what society says is righteous or just and instead follow the truth God reveals to you. The path to righteousness requires consistent and intentional focus, along with the discipline to overcome your flesh. The enemy doesn't scream in your face; he whispers little excuses and lies that pervert the truth.

Everyone's journey through faith reveals different truths and lessons, each one perfectly designed by God, the ultimate engineer, to carve out our unique path. I feel deeply that God has called me to share my journey of faith, not because I feel qualified, but because I believe there's power in testimony. Sometimes, one small part of someone's story can spark a fire in another's heart, motivating them to keep going. I wish I could say my faith journey has been full of only joy, light, and peace. While I've experienced all of those, it has also come with deep sadness, pain, and intense frustration.

I'm a truth-seeker at heart. I spend much of my time researching and learning concepts that reshape how I see the world. I strongly believe in "trying things on" to see if they bring value to my life. Sometimes this leads to powerful revelations; other times, it leads to more questions. I know that everyone's faith walk looks different. I often get frustrated that I can't just take things at the surface level, I have to dig deep and truly understand them. But I believe that's part of my calling: to inspire others to align with their truth through God. Jeremiah 29:13 says, "You will seek me and find me when you seek me with all your heart." That verse brings deep conviction to my heart as I reflect on my own intense seeking for God's truth in my life.

This calling has made me question many choices in my life. Three years ago, I was led to go back to college, something I had no plans to pursue. In fact, when I started, I didn't expect to take much from it, which sounds a bit contrite. Mostly, I felt frustrated about starting something new that would require a complete shift in mindset. But this is where my faith and education journey began to completely reshape the "truth" I had been unraveling for the past eight years.

I grew up in the Catholic faith, and as a child, I didn't feel like the love of God was made a priority. Instead, I perceived fear, fear of eternal damnation, of constant sin, of falling short. That focus never drew me closer to God. One idea that truly sent me into panic was the thought of eternal life. While some see it as a beautiful promise of heaven, I could only imagine it as a never-ending void. The word forever... forever... forever... echoed in my mind like Squints' famous line in The Sandlot.

This fear and confusion eventually led me into deep deception, disguised as the love-and-light world of... drumroll please... New Age Spirituality. I was deeply immersed in it when I began school for Substance Abuse Counseling and Psychology. I quickly realized that this field often relies on faith, and I certainly didn't expect my beliefs to be challenged so completely. I had been so convinced of "my truth" that I even believed Jesus Christ wasn't God, but just an advanced human sent to show us our potential. A pit forms in my stomach as I write that. But if I can't be completely honest about the deception I experienced, why should you trust me?

I know without a doubt that God made you for a reason. I also know the pain
that grips your heart as you look at the brokenness in this world. God created you with purpose. He knows every hair on your head and loves you unconditionally. So many lies are fed to us to disconnect us from Him. The pain and suffering we see are the results of God's absence, not His doing. For a long time, guilt and shame kept me from pursuing a real relationship with God. I thought, Why would He want this broken, sinful woman? But the answer is simple, and it changed my life:

> ## Romans 5:8
>
> **"But God demonstrates His own love for us in this: While we were still sinners, Christ died for us."**

Jesus wants you now, not when you feel pure or good enough. He wants you in your crucified form, just as you are, right where you are. If you want to grow closer to God and discover your true identity through Christ, let's walk that journey together. You have a voice that needs to be heard. Let's put the microphone in your hand. You have questions, a hunger for truth, and a desire to deepen your faith. God loves teamwork, and He most certainly loves you and me. Let's amplify that love. My only goal is to inspire you to grow in your faith, build your relationship with God, and seek Jesus in everything you do. I'm grateful you're here, and I'm so glad you have the desire to find your truth.

Chapter One

Sin, Hell & Salvation.... Oh my

Let's just get straight to the heart of the story! This one is going to be a deep one, something that I am still tackling and truly deepening my understanding of. Growing up in the Catholic religion, I felt the focus was mainly on sin and hell. This is my own reflection and experience; I know others do not share the same account, and that is ok! I just felt like God's love and salvation were not something I found in church. I don't know if that is because so much time is spent talking about repentance, mortal sin, and hell that the grace of God got drowned out? To me, I felt like I was constantly cataloging my sin, ranking it from bad to oooh, you are going to hell now! The thought of dying and going to hell was just too much for my extremely inquisitive mind. Throughout my childhood, I knew I had a healthy conscience of right and wrong; my moral compass was working well. But it didn't come without consequences; I became my own worst critic.

I spent so much time analyzing myself, my actions, and the influence of my peers. I don't know and can't honestly remember if I felt a strong connection to God in my youth. While I now know that, of course, God, the Lord, and the Holy Spirit were with me every step of the way. Back then, I felt like I was navigating youth alone. We were taught the ten commandments and had to memorize them, and if you broke one, you had to confess your sins to the priest. This felt like torture to me; not only did I not want to fully tell the truth, but I also had to figure out a way to soften the blow of what I thought was my ticket to hell. Now, as you are reading, you might think that I was out there just tearing up the streets doing awful things. And you might laugh when I tell you some of the sins I confessed that I thought were the end of me. Just to name a few, these were things like swearing, not listening to my parents, and being rude to a friend.

I have come to understand that our sins don't need ranking; they don't need categorizing; they simply need repentance, which I am happy to do now. So, what changed from my youth to now? My relationship with Jesus, God and the Holy Spirit has grown tremendously. The grace of God now leads my heart, and not the fear of hell or Satan. I need to bring us back to really understand the depth of my growth in faith and the winding road it has been. Childhood for me was good; I was happy, active, and healthy. I spent much of my time outside, playing sports, hanging out with my friends and also a lot of time analyzing the world. Fast forward to today, and not much has changed, except that now I am watching my kids play sports and spending time with my family.

I believe my parents did a good job of laying the foundation of faith for me; they brought me to church, I was receiving the seven sacraments as I was supposed to, and my mom talked to me about God.

I realize now why I felt like I was consistently ranking things and keeping a tab of right and wrong. Receiving the seven sacraments is essentially stamping your ticket to God's grace in the church's eyes. It feels as though we are saying, if I do this and don't do that, then I am saved, I am good enough to enter those pearly gates we all yearn to see. This is also why I felt like I wouldn't see those pearly gates, because at some point, I would mess up badly enough to stamp my ticket to hell. This was a terrifying thought, and oddly enough, one that didn't push me closer to God. Because it felt like I could never be good enough to receive God's grace, I felt that I had to collect enough good evidence that I could then present it to God and hope that he would give me his grace.

This belief system is enough to drive anyone away from God, because how could you ever be good enough to present yourself to the Almighty, omnipresent, all-knowing, all-powerful Heavenly Father? You can't be good enough by trying to be good enough. This is where Yahweh, Jesus, Yeshua, the Lamb of God, the Way, the Truth, and the Life, the King of Kings and the Lord of lords saves us. When you begin to understand the crucifixion and the blood of Christ, you start to truly live. I didn't have this knowledge and understanding the way I do now. That is why I felt I could never be good enough to earn God's grace. You are not meant to travel this road alone, and one of the weapons the enemy uses the most.

Separation from God IS hell, both on earth and in the spiritual realm. The enemy wants you to believe that your problems are unique, that no one else could be going through what you are going through.

When Christ died for our sins, he ripped the veil that separated God from humanity because of our sin. He gave us eternal life and direct access to God, the most beautiful, sacred gift we could ever receive. God loved us so much that he sent his only son to suffer, die and be resurrected. That is why the enemy fights so hard to keep us separated from God. If we truly internalize his deep love and identity through him, we will bring heaven to earth. And Satan wants nothing more than to keep hell spewing its hate and violence around the world. I believe that is what kept me feeling separated from God growing up, the constant lies that I would never be good enough for God, the constant battle of seeking truth, but only finding half of it. This battle followed me into my teenage years, where some of my darkest battles would be fought.

Going through your formative teenage years is a battle in itself; our brains are developing in a way that allows courage and heavy experimentation with dangerous activities. I want to discuss the psychology behind it, because that is a passion of mine, it was also my major, and I believe that when you can dissect what is happening on both a spiritual and physical level, you understand it deeper. The prefrontal cortex is still under construction during your teenage years, which controls decision making, impulse control, and evaluating risk and consequences. Because of this, you are much more likely to act on impulse, emotion and take risks, which can be a good thing, as well as it's God's way of allowing us to grow and learn new things. However, of course, it also opens us up to dangerous things. I know, though, personally, the holy spirit was with me when I experimented with the actions that opened me up to potentially dangerous consequences. I knew this because of how I felt. When Jesus tells us to love our neighbors as ourselves, what we also fail to realize is how we treat ourselves is just as important.

For me treating others with kindness and seeing them in the way God made them was much easier than giving myself the same grace. I kept myself under such intense pressure that it actually pushed me into situations that caused me immense pain. I was also trying to figure out who I was, what my identity should be and the beliefs that would shape me into the person I was becoming. Combine all of this with the enemy infiltrating our society to normalize sin and corruption, and it's the perfect storm for separation from God. By believing that grace is earned and not given freely, growing up can be excruciating because you are essentially keeping a list of your wrongdoings, genuinely believing that it is going to be really hard for God to love you exactly as you are.

To escape that intense pressure of "being good enough" for God to love and save you, unfortunately, many people can turn to substances to help cope with the pain. For me, this became true in high school, what felt like a normal part of growing up turned into escaping reality. I remember my senior year of high school when a tragic accident took the life of one of my classmates.

That was the beginning of me coming face to face with mortality; before that, as many teenagers do, we believe we are invincible. That nothing bad can happen to us. It was also when I felt true anxiety for the first time, and the first time I would use alcohol to numb it. I wish I knew back then what I know now; I would use that extremely vulnerable time in my life to explore my relationship with God. Our ticket to heaven isn't bought by all of our actions; it is through the building of our relationship with God, the Holy Spirit, and Jesus.

It makes so much more sense when you think of it like that, because what if someone who hardly ever talked to you came to your house and said, "Alright, I am here to spend all of eternity with you, I said all of the right things, and followed the ten commandments." You would think they were crazy, because they never spent any time getting to know you and building a lasting relationship with you. They didn't tell you their fears, doubts, and dreams. They didn't ask you to be a constant presence in their life, they didn't ask for your guidance, for your wisdom, or for your grace. They just showed up one day, thinking they would spend the rest of their lives with you.

This is why salvation cannot be earned but rather is deliverance from sin and eternal separation from God. It is THROUGH a restored RELATIONSHIP with God through Jesus Christ. Jesus gave His life so that we could build our eternal relationship with God! No more would we have to use a priest to atone for our sins.

> *"At that moment, the curtain of the temple was torn in two from top to bottom (Matthew 27:51)."*

Jesus removed that barrier for us! But it is our responsibility to build that relationship. You are no longer an outsider, but a child of God. Jesus doesn't want you to clean yourself up to receive his love and grace. He wants you in your crucified form, wherever you are and whatever that looks like.

Imagine if everyone grew up feeling and knowing this truth?? The pain of feeling separation from God or not being worthy enough of his love wouldn't be true the way it can be now. The focal point wouldn't be on hell, sin, and separation, but rather on love, God, and our relationship with the kingdom of heaven. As I navigated my life after high school, I found myself with a decision to make: what would I do? Who did I want to be? This journey took me 1300 miles back to my home state of Montana. The journey didn't pan out the way my mom so desperately wanted it to. She wanted me to experience more and to venture away from home. I made it for a couple of months, and then I went back to Wisconsin.

Throughout this time, I spent much of it in my own head, learning to rely on myself as a young adult, while still needing the support and guidance of my parents. But in true new adult form, I of course knew what I thought was best for myself. Whether or not it would be. You can't see this truth until you are older and have grown in wisdom. It is even harder the second go round, watching your children go through the same "new" adult experience. Now my prayers are for my children to grow in their relationships with God, and to keep them safe and healthy. I know God will work out all of the other details of their lives.

For me, it was important to help them understand the difference between religion and having faith in God. Knowing who God is and growing in faith is the foundation of hope that carries you through life. I wanted them to grow up learning the love of God and not the fear of hell or sin. Not because I want to condone sin, but because they need to know God's grace covers them. We spend much of our time instructing our kids right from wrong, and rightfully so, but it shouldn't be at the cost of their faith. I don't want them to ever feel the way I did, that I could never be or do enough to spend eternity with God. I know I cannot fight their battles or take away their pain or struggles. But I can share the experiences I had and help give insight that hopefully allows them some hope.

Hell can be spent right here on earth if you live life separated from God. Jesus talked about heaven and earth passing away, but never will his word pass away. Jesus also talks about bringing heaven to earth, right in the Lord's Prayer,

"Your kingdom come, your will be done on earth as it is in heaven (Matthew 6:10)."

This speaks to me to live out heaven's values right now, here on earth, exemplifying love, peace, healing, and forgiveness. Jesus embodied heaven on earth; just think of all the miracles he performed, healing the sick, raising the dead, and casting out demons. Jesus didn't just come to bring people to heaven; he came to bring heaven to the people, and through us to the world.

Jesus knew what we were all capable of, and through the gift of the Holy Spirit, we would never have to be alone. We would have the guidance of the greatest counselor to bring us through all of our storms, through our highs, lows, triumphs, and defeats. We are made in the image of our father, who knows who we are deep at our core. He loved us before we were born, and continues to love us through all our striving. Make no mistake, there is an intense spiritual battle going on that we don't see. But we absolutely feel it. Our souls are in high demand, and through generational iniquities, patterns, and traumas, Satan has gained access to us as far back as three or four generations. This is why breaking those generational patterns is so important, so that our children do not have to go through what we did. We can be the example that changes the path for others, which opens the door for healing.

I share all of this not to scare you, but to give you hope, to put on the armor of God, the breastplate of righteousness, the belt of truth, the shoes of the Gospel of peace, the shield of Faith, the helmet of Salvation and the Sword of the Spirit.

This isn't a one-time occurrence; this is an everyday mindset, one that equips and prepares you spiritually. You are not fighting for victory, but from the victory Jesus already won.

Every day we fight to bring heaven to earth, every day we fight against Satan and the kingdom of hell. But I don't want you to fight from a place of fear, I want you to fight for love, from a place of salvation and from a knowing that you are covered by God's grace. We have been deceived numerous times into believing that our differences define us and separate us into categories that make us who we are. These categories keep us divided; they allow others to focus on our differences. God wants us to see each other as he sees us. The best part about this is we do not need to hold judgements against others. We can hold onto our values and know that we never have to worry about judgement because only our father can do that.

The heavy burden of either criticizing ourselves or others was never meant for us to carry. While nailed to the cross, after Jesus was beaten, mocked, spit on, with his organs and bones exposed he let out the most heart wrenching statement,

> "Father, forgive them, for they know not what they do, (Luke 23:34)."

That kind of love is extremely hard for us to truly understand, and that is why only God should be left to judge us. That kind of love is what saved us; that kind of love brings heaven to earth. That kind of love is always enough to cover us.

That is also why it is so important for us to forgive and to repent, because repentance isn't what you think it is. Repentance actually means to change your mind; the original Greek word for repentance is metanoia, which literally means to change one's mind or to turn around mentally (Liddell, H. G. & Scott, R. 1996). Repentance is, quite literally, to change your mind, allowing God to reveal His truth about your situation. Satan only feeds you lies, shame and guilt. This is why when you are stuck in a feeling of unworthiness, you are disconnected from God. God never sees you in that light, no matter what you have done, he wants you to repent, to change your mind and to restore your relationship with him. I hope this chapter has helped you to overcome some of your limiting beliefs on sin, hell, and restoration of your relationship with God. Although we can never have the level of forgiveness that Jesus had, we can have a fraction of it. And that fraction will transform not only our lives but the lives of others.

CHAPTER Two

Jesus, He Is the Redemption Story.

The next phase of my life would bring me through some of the highest highs and the lowest lows. As I navigated life as a young adult, not yet rooted in my own identity or truly knowing anything about who I wanted to be, I often found myself lost. I was deeply wounded from a traumatic experience in my high school years that left me feeling never worthy enough. I know this led me to the need to feel worthy and loved in ways that could never fulfill me. Attention from men or being the life of the party. Things that give you a small, fleeting feeling of being someone. The crazy thing was, I also hated the attention from men; I desperately wanted to be seen for my true self and not just objectified. I look back now, and I just want to hug and hold that version of me and help her to understand who she truly is through the eyes of God. But Satan did his best work on me back then.

I found myself with a stable job, an apartment, a boyfriend, and a puppy. I know I was desperately seeking meaning in my life. I wanted to feel valued, worthy and like I was achieving something. In this period of my life, I didn't have a close relationship with God; I believed there was a God, but I was in a season of life that felt like I was in a constant search for something. But I didn't know what that was. I realize now that if I had a relationship with Jesus, I wouldn't have felt so inadequate, but in my stubbornness to be independent, I kept struggling alone.

I discovered I was pregnant just a few weeks after we brought home our puppy. I was excited but scared as I was just on the cusp of turning twenty. Little did I know having my first child would completely change the direction of my life. Becoming a mom would give me a new sense of self, but also a renewed focus. The first few months were really hard; I had never had to care for someone in such a way that required all of my attention. The love I felt for her was unlike anything I had ever experienced, and I knew that I would live the rest of my life trying to become a better person for her.

I decided that I would go to school for cosmetology. I thought this would give me a way to expand my horizon and experience success. It was during this time my marriage would begin to stumble. We were just kids when we met, I had moved across the country at such a tender age. Looking back, I realized what I needed was true friendship that I had left behind in Montana. In my most tender, formative years, I would be left reeling from an experience that no teenager should have to experience.

This would leave wounds that I am just now fully healing through my relationship with Jesus. I had a prayer life, but it often included asking for things and praying for things to be resolved. Little did I know the consequences of praying for things like strength. When we pray for strength or patience, just like building a muscle, we don't just receive the thing we are asking for. We have to build that "muscle" through experiences or repetition.

As hard as it may be to go through these experiences, they truly are meant to refine us into the person who can handle challenges. The best, most beautiful part is, God doesn't want us to do this alone. In fact, when you learn to rely on God to guide you, instead of being triggered into pulling away, that is when your life changes. That is the moment that you begin to truly embrace that you are NEVER alone. The enemy uses the fact that when challenges or pain arises in our lives, we feel like we have been abandoned by God. What we fail to realize is that we usually abandon God in those moments. I remember so vividly one morning as I sat speaking to God, and I had to get up for a moment, I said I will be right back, don't leave me. To which he replied, "We never leave you, we are always here, you are the one who disconnects from us."

It was in that moment that I realized I was in control of building my relationship with God, the Holy Spirit, and Jesus. But spoiler alert, this was years after I had gone through some of the hardest challenges of my young adult life. As I was learning to be a mother, a wife, and a student, little did I know that those roles would be the fuel that I needed to keep moving forward in my darkest moments.

I believe that even in the moments we aren't actively building our relationship with God, he is always at work in our lives. He knows every single detail, and while we have free will, his guidance is so much stronger than we can even fathom. I continued my faith through the Catholic church, and like I said, a prayer life that wasn't built on building a relationship, but rather asking for things through prayer.

I don't mean that asking for things through prayer is wrong, but it doesn't leave the door open for God to respond. We, as parents, guide our children to help them, especially in the beginning, to basically stay alive. We feed them, change them, hold them, and love them. As they grow and become more independent, they become less and less dependent on us to provide direct care. This is completely different than our relationship with God as our father. As we grow, we need God's guidance MORE, not less. But of course, for many, the opposite can happen. I don't believe this is by chance; I believe the enemy is hard at work at infiltrating religion with false narratives. While community and mentorship are an extremely helpful part of growing your faith, repentance isn't reliant upon anyone but yourself and God.

Thinking of God as your father and allowing him to be an active parent in your life gives you unconditional love and support that we just can't match anywhere else. I didn't have this relationship with him in the beginning; I had an awareness of God and a faith that he was real. But that was enough then, and that was where I was. As life progressed, and I added two more beautiful children to my life, I was still struggling with my marriage.

Meeting your spouse at the age of fourteen, while experiencing extremely traumatic experiences, comes with emotional triggers that can be excruciating. It was as though the enemy sent the attacks through my ex-husband to say the things that hurt me to my core. There came a point where I knew I couldn't carry on the way I had been, but taking the leap to change my life was terrifying. How would I support three young children? The life I thought I had as a mother and wife was crumbling and so was my faith.

I began battling terrible anxiety that kept me up at night, I felt alone, and I wondered if I would ever feel hope again. It felt like I was being consumed with pain as I sat with the failure of my marriage. I wanted to have a family. It was the pride and joy of my life, and to have that ripped apart was devastating. I was turning to everything else but God to help pull me through. I was stumbling through this moment of life and felt like a wreck. I wish that this version of me knew where life would take us, that we would pick the pieces back up, rebuild, and become the person we always knew we could. I would tell her about the man I would meet, who would help me rebuild a life I could only dream of, about the beautiful red-haired boy we would have, who would complete our family. I would tell her how I earned a degree in psychology, like I also wanted to do, that I wrote two books, now three and that I ran a marathon, and got to run a half-marathon through Lambeau field. Most importantly, I would tell her that our relationship with God is stronger than it ever has been. That I gave my life to Jesus, and he has healed so many parts of me that I tell anyone who will listen.

But I couldn't tell her that yet because it hadn't happened. My kids were the one thing that kept me going. I held on through the pain and uncertainty because of them. This journey of faith is an ongoing path that is still being walked as I type. Reliving the hardest moments of your life is not easy; it takes courage and faith that by sharing your story, you might be able to give someone else the courage to share theirs. I ask frequently for Jesus to heal me as I relive the memories. I think the hardest part is that I felt so alone in these moments, yet I know I wasn't. The darkness pulls you in, suffocating you, penetrating your mind to believe that no one else is or has ever felt the way you are feeling. This is how the enemy works: those seemingly quiet thoughts of shame, guilt, worry, and doubt pull you; they become bigger and bigger until you are consumed.

The silent suffering ends up taking lives; it casts its shadow and encompasses you until depression and anxiety envelop you. Do NOT suffer alone. Do not believe the lies that you are the only one who feels this way. Even if you think you are alone, I promise Jesus is there holding you up and fighting against demons you can't see. In your weakest moments, you actually are your strongest because you have to be. I believe various parts of you break off to protect you during traumatic experiences. Your soul can become fractured during these moments; it is like pieces of our identity, splintering off to survive the pain. But God never leaves those pieces behind.

Psalm 34:18, "The Lord is close to those who are crushed in spirit."

You may not know where every fragment is, but God does.

Healing doesn't mean going back to who you were before; it means allowing Jesus to make you whole again in Him, which leads us to exploring false prophets and fake healing modalities, which we will discuss in a later chapter. It seems to provide glimmers of hope and light, but it doesn't give you lasting healing. Agape is the Greek word, described in the Amplified Bible as not so much a matter of emotion, as it is of doing things for the benefit of another person, that is, having an unselfish concern for another and a willingness to seek the best for another." This kind of love is divine and can be hard for humans to convey. The act of doing things solely for the benefit of another person, without any regard for yourself, is rare.

This concept, I believe, is only conveyed through Jesus Christ; he restores us. He allowed his own body to be broken, so that our souls could be made whole. That is the ultimate act of agape. Jesus knew the cross he would bear, but chose to give his whole life to God. He was tempted by Satan; he knew what he would have to endure but still chose us. This is why only Jesus can give us lasting healing; this is why even in your darkest moments, when you feel completely alone, you are not. He is holding you through it. He, without a doubt, held me through these moments, even when I felt like everything was being ripped apart. As God would guide me, I decided to take a trip to visit my brother who was working in Kansas at the time. Little did I know I would meet the man that is now my husband. I want to share the story of how someone can hold space for you to heal, without doing any of the work for you.

When I met him, neither of us had any intention of forming a relationship. He was working in Kansas, about nine hundred miles away from me, and I was a single mom of three small children. Most accurately, I didn't believe anyone would love me enough to meet me where I was in my brokenness. I also was at a point where I didn't value myself enough to believe I was capable of receiving love. But through all of my pain, he saw me; he saw me when I felt no one else did. He saw me in a way that valued who I was at my core. I was so bruised from feeling as though no one could ever love me as I was. He loved me in a way I had never been loved before, without jealousy or in a possessive way, but in a way that made me feel he was proud to love me.

In my brokenness, I failed to realize that Jesus loved me; he saw me for who I truly was. When we don't feel capable of receiving love, that is the enemy deceiving us that in our sin we are unwanted. Jesus always wants us; in fact, Jesus actively pursues you in your darkest moments. He always meets you where you are. Jesus walked through pain, betrayal, temptation and death, the full human experience. He fully understands your suffering and the hardship of the human experience. He loves you exactly as you are, even when you think no one else can.

This new relationship gave me the courage to pick myself back up, he didn't heal me, and in fact, he would have to be a part of my past trauma that would resurface over and over again. It was anything but rainbows and butterflies, but he was a huge part of my ability to heal. I knew God paved the path to him. To have someone love you through all of your darkness is a true gift, someone that isn't God, I would like to clarify. Even though I had someone that eased the pain of loneliness I had so much healing work that needed to be done. This would flare up so many times in our relationship. During this time, I had the opportunity to open my own salon. This gave me purpose and thankfully a way to support myself and my children.

Slowly, I was forming a new future; my nights and days weren't constantly consumed by anxiety. I don't think that things drastically changed, but my focus shifted. I wasn't consumed by hopelessness but a glimmer of hope for a new future. I was learning to grow a business, while being a mother and forming a long-distance relationship. This alone consumed a large part of my energy, and even though I was not actively working on building my relationship with Jesus, he was hard at work behind the scenes in my life. I believe the experiences we go through can be used to build our resiliency, which positions us to better handle challenges. Going through hardships while solely relying on yourself leaves you with resistance towards going through them again.

When people say they turn to Jesus in hardships, I didn't get what they meant. How was I supposed to give up the reins? How was I supposed to let go of control over my life, when I was in charge of running a business and taking care of three children? I didn't know what it really meant to turn to God when life was blowing up in my face. It used to sound like asking God to "fix" whatever circumstances were causing me frustration. I have learned that this looks like surrendering to God, asking him to show you what you need—asking him to give you the mind of Jesus to see the situation clearer.

Most importantly, turning to God in the moments you are triggered, asking him to take away your trigger and replace it with the truth.

We do not understand the power of learning the truth about ourselves as God sees us. There is an unbelievable strength that comes from learning to see yourself as Father God sees you. To have him show you the lies the enemy has planted within the triggers you have. That is the truth I have uncovered in my faith: when triggered, I no longer allow the trigger to consume me; I turn directly to God, I ask for guidance, support, and protection. I consistently plead the blood of Jesus over myself, my husband, my children, my house, my dogs, my bank accounts, my business, my cars, and everything under my stewardship. This type of protection begins to grow and builds around not only your soul but everything under your care.

Your journey in faith is yours and yours alone to walk. No one can tell you how to build it. No one can tell you what is best for you but Jesus. No one else has the authority to judge you for your journey. At the beginning of being saved, it can be easy to become consumed by right and wrong, as evidenced by the Ten Commandments. But quickly I realized Jesus calls us to love others, through their sin, because we are all sinners. Do not withhold forgiveness, because one day you just might need to be forgiven. Resentment makes your soul tired and grow weary. It pulls you down from true alignment with Jesus. Just as Jesus followed me through my darkness, died for my sins, and restored me from my brokenness to a wholeness only he can provide,

Matthew 6:14 reminds us, "For if you forgive other people when they sin against you, your heavenly Father will also forgive you. But if you do not forgive others their sins, your Father will not forgive your sins."

Isaiah 43:2, "When you pass through the waters, I will be with you; and when you pass through the rivers, they will not sweep over you. When you walk through the fire, you will not be burned; the flames will not set you ablaze."

God doesn't say if you walk through hard things. He says when. And in those moments, He is with you. Jesus isn't waiting on the other side of your redemption story; he is the redemption. He walks through it with you, even when you think you are walking alone. He is never waiting for you to get it right or get it together to come to you. He is with you in the storm, even when you feel like you have failed, even when you feel numb, even when you no longer know how to pray. He is always there, steadfast, loving, and faithful.

CHAPTER
Three

Counterfeit Light and Love

By now my life was filled with taking care of my three small children, owning, and operating a salon and fumbling through my relationship. The hardest part about all of it was that I was still so deeply wounded that my patterns and behaviors displayed the pain I held internally. I so desperately wanted to feel worthy, even after I had a new relationship with someone who loved me deeply, while I was running my own business and had three children, I loved with all of my heart. What was missing? My relationship with Jesus. Plain and simple. If you are searching for worth and value by achieving things, or through relationships or titles, you will search forever. True fulfillment comes from our true identity as daughters and sons of God. Made in his image. That is our truth. Our society has become so loud, leading us to believe that materialistic items, titles of success and how many likes and comments we receive equate to our value as a human being.

This can be completely overwhelming, and something that we can never get enough of, or do enough to be "good enough." It is a constant comparison game, a highlight reel of our wins. But what about our losses? What about the moments we feel incredibly alone? We are led to believe that it's outdated to believe in long-term commitment to someone. That partying is a way of life, and that we can change who God designed us to be. It is so easy now to see the enemy hard at work behind the scenes, pulling the puppet strings on media and every system that was designed. How can we find fulfillment and peace when focusing on things in this world? Without Jesus, it is impossible. You might be able to win or succeed, but what are you winning at? Are they really from God?

Many people carry emotional pain that didn't start with them; it has been passed down through generations. These generational patterns can include things like unhealthy coping mechanisms, addiction, emotional dysregulation, or repeated cycles of trauma. Without realizing it, people often live out beliefs and behaviors they have inherited from their parents, grandparents, or caregivers. For me, it became clear that I wanted to make a change for my children. After we welcomed my fourth and final baby, a little red-haired, blue-eyed boy, I was shocked to see his hair color when he was born. I became extremely interested in the power of thoughts, metaphysics, and holistic health.

In theory, it sounds great. I finally felt like I was starting to make sense of things, and a new way of thinking entered my brain. I started to feel a tug at putting well-being on the top of my list. I had lived in the exhausted, anxious, and stressed-out version of myself for so long. Was it time to finally start exploring wellness? I wanted to become a better mom and version of myself; I started taking steps to take care of myself. For the first time in a long time, I had found friends who were also prioritizing health. It matters who you surround yourself with; if you are around people who have goals and dreams and are actively pursuing them, it can be contagious. I started to feel a sense of hope and found motivation for my future in a way that I hadn't connected with before.

And then just as fast as this new beginning was taking shape, it started to crash back down. My husband was offered a new job in a town about an hour from where we were currently. I wanted my children to go to school there, as it could offer them new opportunities; however, this possibility came to a halt. At this point in time, my ex-husband and I were not in agreement with our children changing schools, and it ended up in a court battle. This alone was exhausting, draining and so stressful. The judge decided it was in their best interest to stay in the schools they were in, but with no other direction. The feeling I had that a stranger was able to decide what was best for my kids broke me. I remember that day so vividly; my heart felt like it had been ripped apart.

We moved and the schedule we had with the kids was hard. I hated having them go back and forth before they had spent almost every night with me. It was as if my entire soul had been ripped in half. The pain was all-consuming, and I had a tough time escaping it. I remember the night after my kids had gone to their dads, I got in my car, driving around, wishing desperately for the pain I was feeling to go away. I drove back, got to the steps, fell to my knees and I begged God, "Please either take this pain, or take me, because I can't do this anymore." The pain had consumed me, and I was believing all the lies that the enemy was feeding me.

The next morning, I woke up, and I knew I couldn't keep living the way I was. I felt as though the Lord was telling me I had to find gratitude for the moments I had with my kids, or I would continue to live in this pain. I started focusing on the time I had with them, instead of being consumed with anxiety about the time they would leave. You see, the enemy uses our pain and fear to control us, to confuse us into thinking we are stuck or alone. When you find your identity through God, it is game over for Satan. You will still be attacked, but those attacks don't have the same effect. You were formed in your mother's womb deliberately by God, for a purpose, with a purpose.

The beautiful truth, even in your most painful moments, is that Jesus is always with you.

> **Isaiah 41:10, "Don't be afraid, for I am with you. Don't be discouraged, for I am your God. I will strengthen you and help you. I will hold you up with my victorious right hand."**

You can look back at your toughest hour, and you know Jesus was there in spiritual battle protecting you against the enemies of darkness. I began to live for the present day, learning to find joy again. It was also around the time I started to learn about the power of your thoughts and building a positive mindset.

I began reading books that opened me up to the concept that you are not your thoughts, but rather you are the awareness of your voice. I started to focus intently on affirmations, vision casting and fell headfirst into this newfound spirituality. I wrote on index cards the goals I had, my desires and dreams. I read them morning, noon, and night. Looking back, there is a lot of truth to the New Age movement; however, they

take Jesus out of the equation. The power of your focus and thoughts ARE very important. Your brain is a powerful tool, designed by God. It is primarily designed to keep you alive and procreate. That is why it is your job to be the gatekeeper of what you allow in. New age spirituality promises healing, peace, and enlightenment, but without surrender. It offers a form of truth that centers you as your own God, not Christ as Lord.

I became certified as a Master Life Coach and fell head over heels in love with self-development and mindset. I was deep in the New Age, and I won't lie, there are truths in it, and that is why it is so appealing. You learn about energy, inner healing, meditation, vibration, and intention, things that all sound aligned with peace and growth. But here is where the deception creeps in: you hear things like "trust the universe." Or "thank you, universe, for your guidance."

And yet you don't realize you are trusting and praising God's creation. The universe isn't the one guiding, blessing, and creating life; GOD is. The biggest deception in the New Age movement is that you are an extension of God; you are here as a spark of God experiencing life.

After you die, you go back and are basically "absorbed" back into mass consciousness. This poises you as the source of your own healing; it relies on you and not Christ for your healing. It replaces the need for Jesus with the universe or source energy. I began to explore techniques like Reiki, past-life regression, and medium readings. Reiki teaches you that you are channeling universal life force energy to heal others. I remember hearing the word light worker and
feeling like I had found my purpose. When I say I went DEEP into this, I mean it. I spent thousands of hours listening to podcasts, audiobooks, and "meditating" and connecting with my spirit guides. I learned about things like soul contracts, karma, and reincarnation.

I remember starting to believe that it didn't really matter if you experienced good or bad things, because you were just going to come back and relearn the lesson you didn't learn in this life. I believed that we are all energetic beings emitting frequencies that bring you up the scale in dimension that connects you with beings or entities at those certain levels. Now there is truth that we have spirits and souls. Your soul is your essence and who God created first, before you were formed in your mother's womb. Your soul makes you uniquely you, designed by God.

Who you are was specifically engineered, detail by tiny detail, to be encoded with the attributes specific to your purpose. God is the master creator, who orchestrates every single thing that happens. He is the ultimate creator. Satan does not create anything; he can only twist, distort, mimic, or counterfeit what God has already made. This is exactly what New Age is built on.

Satan took God's blueprint and made it counterfeit, so that while you can find some healing, it never lasts and is never found through Jesus. I believe this is why so many people have taken refuge in this movement; it gives them a sense of power, a feeling of importance, and a direction. I know for me it distorted my view of God, with ideas such as God is a woman, God isn't a being, God is all of us. Do you see the confusion in all of this? Do you see how it takes you out of alignment with who God created you to be?

John 1:3, "All things were made through him, and without him was not anything made that was made."

I also spent hours connecting to what I had learned and believed were my spirit guides. At first, it seemed so true. It felt like there were these brilliant, advanced spirits, giving me guidance and insight. But these spirit guides are counterfeit, leading you from point A to point B, without true spiritual direction from God.

I had no idea that I was opening myself up to the kingdom of darkness. I genuinely believed everything was love and light. But the enemy is the master of deception, even though I hate giving him credit for anything, he truly has earned this title.

I continued this journey for so long, to the point where I could never know or learn enough to satisfy myself. It was this never-ending quest to finally find the answer that would enlighten me enough to feel fulfilled. I remember at one point in my journey telling someone that Jesus was just a normal being who came to show us what we are all capable of. Yep, I said that, and I have repented for that. I take full responsibility for this statement, but I also believe this is evidence of the power of Satan's deception. I believe in our worthiness and believe we are unbelievably capable of our wildest dreams. But without God, Jesus, and the Holy Spirit we are in the middle of the ocean with no paddle or direction. Our worthiness comes from the fact that we were made in God's image, from the moment we take our first breath, our father has loved us and divinely created us. This alone fills me with a feeling of complete wholeness that the New Age could never provide.

I lived in this space for a long time. During 2020, when the world shut down, I found myself lacking any real motivation. It became wine o'clock every day at 3, when homeschool was officially done. I remember how emotionally drained I became and how physically exhausted I was. In February 2021, I knew I wanted to make a change, not just for my health but for my spiritual and mental health. I decided I would no longer be drinking alcohol. When I first began my sobriety journey, the thought of never having a drink again was daunting. Alcohol has become such a normalized part of our society that it is alcohol served at nearly every event we encounter.

At first, all I could focus on was what I thought I was losing, but what I ended up gaining completely surpassed all of my wildest dreams. I had a newfound focus; I wasn't sick, tired, or anxious. My motivation wasn't waxing and waning, dependent on whether I had had too much "fun" that weekend. No one really talks about the hell that alcohol introduces into your life. It gave me the strength I had been longing for. I was given back so much time. In August 2022, I decided I wanted to pursue substance abuse counseling education. I had never considered going back to school; it just wasn't in my cards. I was going to continue on this spiritual journey, in love and light manifest my way to my desires. But it was exhausting because I was doing it through a counterfeit source. One that depletes your energy, thrives off of your pain and derails true success that can only be found through the Lord.

School was a renewed focus, a path I had not considered before. After I finished my first year, I began working as a substance abuse counselor in training at a residential treatment center. This would be one of the hardest careers I have ever encountered. Hearing the stories from those struggling with addiction was heartbreaking. It was clear to me that the enemy infiltrates society, leading us to substances, false prophets, and lies that take us out of alignment with God. People who go through trauma and abuse are looking for a way to escape the pain that overwhelms them. Just ask anyone who has struggled with or is struggling with substance abuse, and they will tell you about the pain that overtook them. It is too much to handle alone, and then when substances are used to cope, your brain takes over, desperately trying to return to homeostasis.

When you continually use a substance, your brain is flooded with dopamine, which is the feel-good chemical. The terrible part about addiction is that at one point you didn't rely on the drug. Your brain wants to return to balance but it cannot. The more you use it, the more your brain tries to adapt, and that is a living hell to go through. Mental health disorders and addiction go together like storm clouds and lightning. Because of underlying conditions like depression, anxiety, or PTSD, when someone tries to stop using, it leads to many people being triggered into relapse. It felt almost impossible to try to help people recover and stay sober.

The truth is, I knew I couldn't do it alone, but I was still stuck in the New Age spirituality mindset that it didn't matter what they believed in; they just had to believe in something bigger than themselves. The problem is that this still leads you back to the kingdom of darkness, if there is no believe in God or Jesus what does that leave? It leaves room for the enemy to offer temporary solutions that lead you farther into the darkness. There is freedom from addiction; it starts with Jesus.

> **Romans 12:2 reminds us, "Do not conform to the pattern of this world, but be transformed by the renewing of your mind. Then you will be able to test and approve what God's will is, his good and pleasing and perfect will."**

We need to understand that patterns run through generations; it is not enough to only acknowledge the physical world. We must address the spiritual world. We have to understand our authority and covenant with God. Corinthians 10:4, "The weapons we fight with are not the weapons of the world. On the contrary, they have divine power to demolish strongholds." This is why I say that to beat addiction, we need Jesus. He is the ultimate spiritual warrior who heals and brings lasting change. You can fight like hell by yourself, but only Jesus holds the key to defeating the kingdom of darkness.

CHAPTER
Four

Surrendering to Jesus

I quickly realized that the people I was working with felt completely unseen, unworthy and unloved. They had battled the darkness for so long that they forgot what their true identity was. The enemy had taken over and allowed the lies to consume them. How do you keep people from God? By feeding them lies that they are too far gone or that they are unforgivable. I will never forget a night that I got to pour into them, remind them of their true potential. They are so used to being seen as a client, inmate or just another number in the system, this is just another way for their enemy to captivate them to stay in addiction. Being able to see them as human beings with dreams and purpose is the best gift you can give.

When you believe you are unworthy and do not believe that God always loves you and Jesus is always holding you, it is tough to get sober or make a change in your life. It is a terrible feeling to think that you are unworthy or too "sinful" to have God in your life. The enemy's focus is on your relationship with God; if you don't have one, that is the goal. If you are building one, the tactics to distract you come out at every little twist and turn. The next opportunity I took would give me a peek into how the enemy uses perversion to divide people.

After I ended my chapter at the treatment center, I began a role that, while the focus felt right, the message portrayed by the agency was completely misaligned with the values I hold. I thought that I could help people with the skills I had gained. However, God allows us to learn valuable lessons, even if it leads us through pain. This experience was the first time in my life that I felt discriminated against for my beliefs. This experience taught me that sometimes people only see you as someone who holds value and worth if you align with their beliefs. This is a tough lesson to learn, it is one that causes you to feel unworthy. Yet, you are basing these feelings on someone who hasn't aligned with God's will or built a relationship with God.

How do I know this? Because a true follower of Christ doesn't base their value or opinion of you on anything other than you being a child of God. I was filled with anger and frustration over what had happened. I wanted to let go and move forward, but the injustice I felt was so heavy. I was ok with being disliked, but the thought of someone seeing my values as harmful was a feeling I had never felt before. It was the beginning of understanding what Jesus meant when he warns that his followers would be persecuted.

Peter was imprisoned, beaten and crucified upside down. James was killed by a sword, and John was exiled to the island of Patmos.

> **John 15:18-20, "If the world hates you, keep in mind that it hated me first. If you belonged to the world, it would love you as its own. As it is, you do not belong to the world, but I have chosen you out of the world. That is why the world hates you. Remember what I told you: 'A servant is not greater than his master.' If they persecuted me, they would persecute you also."**

I was a lukewarm follower of Jesus at this point of my life, so forgiveness wasn't at the top of my list. I was also completely consumed with an upcoming surgery for my daughter that would correct a hip dealignment that required a very invasive procedure. I tried to hold on and stick it out in this position I was in, but the bitterness and complete frustration I felt soon made me realize I had to leave. I couldn't allow myself to live like this any longer; it was taking a toll on my emotional well-being. The thing that not many people realize though is even after your circumstances change, your thoughts and emotions go with you.

You will have to address the unforgiveness at some point. Because it will follow you, even if you feel the justification to be angry, because it will poison your spirit.

> **Ephesians 4:31-32 tells us to "Get rid of all bitterness, rage, and anger, brawling and slander, along with every form of malice. Be kind and compassionate to one another, forgiving each other, just as in Christ God forgave you."**

In complete honesty, I didn't use the bible as a guidebook for life; I didn't realize that it was the blueprint given to us to live in alignment with God. In New Age the blueprint always come from another person, a spirit guide, a book, a podcast, anywhere that doesn't lead you directly to God.

That meant I wasn't taking direction and guidance from God, Jesus, or the Holy Spirit, and that was why I was constantly left searching for the truth. Just when I thought I had figured out an answer I was left with even more answers. And even when I felt healed, it never lasted. That is what the New Age movement is meant to do: it is meant to deceive people. Sure, you feel like you are becoming an enlightened being, and you have some success in your healing journey. But just as soon as you are triggered, bam, the demons show right back up. There isn't true growth and release from your triggers. The only true way is to use your authority and claim the blood of Jesus over everything under your stewardship. To address and renounce all of the patterns passed down from generations in your family.

If this sounds like New Age, it is because it can only be dealt with in the spiritual realm. Christians that don't understand or attempt to learn about the spiritual side of existence miss out on the full scope of authority and covenant they have with God. God sent Jesus to live a perfect life, something we could never do, and to take the punishment for our sins through his death on the cross. His resurrection conquered death and proved that he has the power to bring eternal life. Because of Jesus's ultimate sacrifice, we are offered forgiveness, freedom, and a restored relationship with God, which is not based on our efforts but on grace. He didn't just come to offer eternal life after death; he came so you can live fully now. He is the way back to truth, peace, and purpose.

But then we are brought to the question that is used in every theology introduction course: "Why does God allow bad things to happen?" Or better yet, if God is all-knowing and all-powerful, why did he create Lucifer knowing he would betray him? God gave us free will; he gave us the ability to choose love, obedience, and trust or to reject it. He didn't create us to be machines or robots; he created us with the freedom to choose. Lucifer was created as a beautiful, powerful angel (Ezekiel 28:12-17), but his pride overcame him, and he wanted to be worshipped like God. This rebellion was of Lucifer's own free will. Even knowing the pain that would come from Lucifer's rebellion, God already had a plan for redemption: **Jesus.**

This is where true accountability comes in, when you acknowledge that while bad things happen, we have to take responsibility to heal, to grow in our relationships with God, Jesus, and the Holy Spirit; otherwise, we are just sitting ducks in a pond. We cannot allow our circumstances to define us and hold us captive, because even when circumstances change, we may not be able. You can blame God, other people, or your situation, but the truth that gives you power back is your ability to pull yourself back up.

The best part about this is that Jesus is waiting for you to come to him in that moment.

Joshua 1:9, "Have I not commanded you? Be strong and courageous. Do not be afraid; do not be discouraged, for the Lord your God will be with you wherever you go."

Strength isn't just about being able to lift heavy objects; it is the courage in the face of fear, knowing God is with you.

This is where my faith was completely changed with the ultimate moment of surrender. As any parent can sympathize with, when your children are in pain, you would give anything to be able to take the pain from them. I was extremely nervous as my daughter and I drove down to Mayo Clinic in Rochester, Minnesota. We were trying to keep things lighthearted and keep our minds off the surgery she was having. We woke up at 5 am to head over to the hospital; the nurse went through all of the pre-operative procedures. They explain all the risks and followed up with how low the chance of them happening is. At 7 am, they moved her into the operating room, and at 7:30, I received a text that the surgery had begun.

Mayo Clinic has a huge subway tunnel system that connects many shops, restaurants, hotels and the various clinics and hospitals. I was walking on the subway back to the hotel to try to help calm my nerves, as the surgery she would undergo was extensive. She had to have her pelvis cut in three places, repositioned, and screwed back together; she had a torn labrum repaired and some bone shaved down. The thought of all that work being done on my 15-year-old daughter was crushing. I spent moments with tears in my eyes, and moments praying to God to watch over her and protect her.

Finally, after what felt like a lifetime , around 4:30, we were able to go back into the recovery room.

This is the moment that crushed me. I have to preface this by addressing the strength and ability to endure pain my daughter has. She had been running for over 2 years on two torn labrums and hip dysplasia. When I saw her, I was so relieved, but that relief quickly turned to a feeling of helplessness. As she woke up, the pain from the boots that had compressed her legs for nine hours had left her calves in excruciating pain. She was crying and in uncontrollable pain. Hearing the nurses talk about the pain medication they were giving her was also scary as she is so petite. Watching her in this state was breaking me. I was stroking her head and begging God to take away her pain.

I remember specifically having to sit down because I felt so lightheaded from the trauma of watching her go through this hell. It was this moment that I truly started to understand I was absolutely powerless without God. I had for so long felt that I had to be strong, courageous and forge my own path. This moment made me realize I am nothing without God. Life has a funny way of breaking you if you don't align with the path God intended for you. I thank God for this moment, not for her pain, but for the realization that God sees what we can't. His plans protect, guide, and lead us back into peace, purpose, and eternal hope.

2 Corinthians 12:9-10, "But he said to me, 'My grace is sufficient for you, for my power is made perfect in weakness.' Therefore, I will boast all the more gladly about my weaknesses, so that Christ's power may rest on me… For when I am weak, then I am strong."

I had never thought that through all of the pain and frustration of the past year, it would lead me to this moment of surrender. I was clinging so tightly to how I thought my life was going to play out that I was living in self-righteousness. Meaning I felt I had to work hard and make things happen that weren't guided by God. I was wearing myself out, and I realized surrender is the way to freedom. I wanted to control my life and the outcome; I wanted things to unfold the way I thought they were meant to. But this moment? The moment I had to watch my daughter go through this extreme challenge was my surrender. After her pain finally got under control, we were brought up to her room, where we would stay for the next few days.

That night, I did not get much sleep as the IV drip machine went off about every 30 minutes. I also had to watch my highly active, healthy daughter struggle to be able to walk. We had to push her left leg forward because she couldn't feel the bottoms of her feet and had a tough time getting her leg to move. She struggled with being so vulnerable and limited in what she could do. I would take a walk when she would sleep because I had to hold it together for her, but when I left, I would call my mom and sob over the phone. To date, that was one of the hardest experiences for me; to watch her go through that was the most helpless feeling.

We were supposed to go home on Friday, but with the limitations of her ability to move, we would stay another night. Saturday, she woke up with extreme nausea that left her bedridden and unable to move.

Sunday, even though she was still sick, God gave her the motivation, and quite honestly, she is as stubborn as they come, to do the things physical therapy needed her to do before they could release us. I felt like I was driving a newborn baby home again, that feeling of being terrified of hitting bumps or doing anything that could potentially hurt her. My daughter is one of the strongest people I know, also the most stubborn, which isn't always easy trying to mother
through. But that stubbornness got her through physical therapy like a champ. Her recovery was so inspiring to watch her go through such pain and challenge. It was also the beginning of my surrendering to the Lord; I could force and make many things happen in my life.

But when it came to my children, having to surrender through the pain, fear and helpless feeling was life-changing. Things in my life didn't magically change overnight, and I still had some belief residue left over from the New Age. Jesus told us in

> **Matthew 17:20, "Truly I tell you, if you have faith as small as a mustard seed, you can say to this mountain, Move from here to there,' and it will move. Nothing will be impossible for you."**

My mustard seed had been planted, and it would take a bit to grow. A mustard seed is tiny, about 1 to 2 millimeters, but it grows to a huge plant; some can grow over six feet tall. Even the smallest step of faith, when planted in trust, can grow into something that impacts not just your life, but the lives of others.

I do not consider myself an expert on anything. The things I do know are that I am incredibly passionate about a holistic well-being mindset, learning, and applying what I have learned to my life. I love to share what I experience, because I have been so blessed by others who do the same. I love that even now, my faith journey is evolving; it is inspiring to look back and see how it has transpired. Even as I write, it is growing from the first sentence written in this book. Faith is the biggest gift we have been given. It grows through pain, beauty, challenges, doubt, and surrender. Faith is defined as complete trust or confidence in someone or something, or a strong belief in God or in the doctrines of a religion, based on spiritual apprehension rather than proof.

Faith can move mountains, but sometimes we are placed on the backside of the mountain, being refined by God to be able to handle the next transition in our lives. We often try to rush things or rely on our limited belief in timing to make us think we are not where we should be. The thing is, we have to use our faith to understand that God's timing isn't late, it's intentional. Sometimes he delays the answer because he's developing the character. The wait is where the real miracle is happening, inside you. God sees the whole picture; we see where we are at. Ecclesiastes 3:11, "He has made everything beautiful in its time."

I have struggled with this feeling for so long, always feeling I should be somewhere other than where I was at. God has given me such a gift by allowing me to learn through my challenges, by surrendering to his will, his way and his guidance, bringing you into alignment with a life that fulfills you.

He has allowed me to experience moments that pushed me into surrendering to his timing. After my daughter's surgery, I was learning to surrender to his timing, and let me tell you, I was learning at the pace of a sloth crossing a road. One moment, I would surrender to his timing, the next, I was crying, begging God to fulfill my dreams and desires. Even just a year ago, if he had given me what I asked for, I would not have the depth of understanding I have now. And in a year from now, it will be completely different too. It is through surrender of control that we are allowed the time to experience the situations we need to. Our humanness is so loud at times that we need to know the how and the why. I am realizing that I don't need to know that, and the feeling of knowing that God has me is unbelievably peaceful. Does this mean I won't have challenges, hardships, and pain? Absolutely not. Challenges will come. Pain is part of this life. But when you trust God in the middle of the storm, something shifts.

The pain doesn't disappear, but it gains purpose; the road doesn't get easier, but you no longer have to walk it alone. Trusting God doesn't mean you won't face the fire; it means the fire won't consume you. It means the valleys become a place of transformation, not defeat. Let God guide you; he isn't waiting on top of the mountain; he's waiting right there with you at the bottom.

Isaiah 43:2, "When you pass through the waters, I will be with you; and when you pass through the rivers, they will not sweep over you. When you walk through the fire, you will not be burned."

Allow God to refine you, allow God to strengthen you, allow God to clear the path so you know which direction to turn. When you get to know God, Jesus, and the Holy Spirit, you get to know the way, the truth, and the life. How long will you hold on before you surrender?

CHAPTER Five

PURPOSE FROM PAIN

God can be present in your life while you are struggling or in pain. It is a misconception that God will never allow pain or challenges into your life. New Age twists the truth and causes many people to ask the question, "Why would a loving God send me to hell to suffer for all eternity"? My question to counter that is, "Where is your responsibility in that question?" God didn't create hell for humans to suffer in; it is through the courts of Heaven and the lack of our acceptance as Jesus as our savior, and the failure to build our relationship with God, the Holy Spirit and Jesus. It is much easier not to believe in Hell or Satan because that takes away accountability for our sins and iniquities. If we have nothing to hold us accountable to or the fear of eternal damnation, what do we have left? An open door for the enemy to infiltrate our lives.

It feels like you are throwing darts at a map but asking questions for a specific area. You may get an answer or guidance, but it is never meant to lead you to your actual destination. That is the deception that is purposefully used by the enemy. At first, it feels so good, so true, so light. It allows you to find a place that religion might not have given you, and you feel like you have found earth-shattering evidence of how to change the world. You might believe you were sent o earth to be a "light worker" to help bring up the vibration so that we can transcend the current dimension and become an enlightened group of beings. This sounds good, or even worthy of spending time on building an understanding.

You might have even heard of the ever-growing concept of Christ consciousness, where Jesus is seen not as a person but as a universal state of higher awareness or enlightenment that anyone can attain. Jesus is seen as an example but not as our savior, not as uniquely divine, but as a spiritual teacher who has demonstrated what we can all become. Everyone has a divine spark, not just Jesus, but we are all gods in some form. It teaches that instead of sin and redemption, we need to awaken to our higher truth, through meditation, our high self or mindfulness. The problem with this is that it redefines Jesus in a way that removes his role as savior, it eliminates sin, repentance, and the need for the cross or the blood of Christ. It feels like a never-ending loop of learning a concept, but still needing more understanding to find the "truth." There is no true peace, and quite honestly, the accountability of following the Ten Commandments is often taken away.

I think this is what makes it so appealing, all the answers are found "within," there is no heaven or hell, or Satan, there is a God, but EVERYTHING is God. As I navigated life with a newfound reliance on Jesus, but still pulled in by the New Age, it felt the same. Nothing was really changing; I still didn't find the answer I had been searching for, and I was still reeling from the lingering residue of the job that had left me feeling completely shaken. I love hearing the stories where people have moments where Jesus comes to them, and they are completely transformed. My story is a little bit different than that; it also isn't nearly as exciting or flashy. It was a series of moments that were breaking me free from the patterns of thoughts that kept me in deception.

Now, it is especially important not to idolize anyone, because the only person we should be putting first is God. However, someone I admired and looked up to started openly talking about her journey from New Age to Jesus. It gave me the courage to begin exploring my relationship with Jesus. It led me to a podcast that explored so many things I had been dying to figure out. This led me to a different podcast that completely changed me. I would like to say it was a sense of peace. But Jesus had other plans; he needed me to understand who we are up against, he wanted me to know that Satan and hell are very real. After I had traumatized myself enough to the point where I wasn't sleeping well, I realized it was time to focus on building my relationship with Jesus.

I had to be broken up first, and let me tell you, it was the most vulnerable I had ever felt. No longer could I pretend to hide behind my ego, because God knows exactly who I am.

He knows all of my thoughts and desires. He knows all of my sins, every single detail, he knows. I could no longer be self-reliant, which was my whole identity; I could always figure it out myself. I would always find a way through because that is who I was. To give that up and now allow God to lead me wasn't easy. I fought him and resisted giving up the "strength" I had fallen back on so many times. Because I had gone through a divorce in my early twenties with three small children, I had built up my armor, but it wasn't the armor of God; it was the armor of self-reliance, also disguised as self-preservation. For so long, I thought I had to be strong enough to make it through life, because if I wasn't, who was going to hold me up? Trauma had deceived me into believing no one else could truly be trusted to back me up.

The enemy KNOWS our weaknesses; he amplifies them, making them stronger and louder. He uses self-reliance as a tool because it takes away our reliance on Jesus. As humans, we were never meant to carry everything; that is why Jesus told us in

Matthew 11:28, "Come to me all who labor and are heavy laden, and I will give you rest."

Take my yoke upon you, and learn from me, for I am gentle and lowly in heart, and you will find rest for your souls. For my yoke is easy, and my burden is light." Jesus is telling you that by asking for him to guide you, your burden will be lightened. The enemy deceives you by accepting that strength is forged through walking through challenges alone.

But I have learned that it isn't strength, that is stupidity. When we have a savior like Jesus waiting for us to turn to him, yet we think in our finite minds and fragile bodies that we can do it better? Yes, I will call that stupidity. But I hope you know that I am addressing myself in those moments of believing I could do it all, and I didn't need anyone to help me. I wanted so badly to help others, but Jesus was calling me to be helped first! I resisted this until I began to open my heart and mind to what the Holy Spirit, God and Jesus were conveying to me. I began reading the bible, something I had attempted many times before. This time was different; I found a version of the bible (amplified version) that allowed me to connect with it in a way I had never been able to before.

I started in the beginning, but something compelled me to eventually begin reading the New Testament. I think this is a pretty relatable feeling that the New Testament is much easier to connect with, and for me personally, it really spoke to me. I was completely devoted and set myself a minimum of ten pages a day. I was faithful to read every day, even if it was just a page, for months. When I finished the New Testament, I was a little bit sad as I knew I would begin reading the Old Testament again. The Holy Spirit prompted me to, in tandem while reading the OT, begin reading the NT again. I couldn't believe the new layers that were appearing to me. This time, I felt like Jesus was speaking to me directly about the blueprint, the blueprint to get to Heaven. People like to attack the bible, even call it fiction, yet the Holy Spirit, Jesus and God have all directed me to the Word of God.

There is a reason non-believers have a tough time reading the bible and would be able to call it fiction. Corinthians 2:14, "The natural person does not accept the things of the Spirit of God, for they are folly to him, and he is not able to understand them because they are spiritually discerned." The Bible reads like a rulebook instead of a love letter, and the biggest reason of all is that they lack the relationship that brings the words to life. Jesus said,

> **"You search the Scriptures because you think that in them you have eternal life; and it is they that bear witness about me, yet you refuse to come to me that you may have life." (John 5:39-40).**

The words do come to life when you actively build your relationship with the Holy Trinity. It does feel like a love letter now to read it; I can now feel Jesus's presence as I read the words that knit the fabric of life together.

Jesus is the way; he showed us this with his life journey. He is the truth; he came to share God's word, and he is the life. He is the very breath we take, and without him, we are lost. The sweetest part of surrendering to Christ was the very thing I needed the most. I had spent so much time in meditation, receiving "guidance" and "visions" from spirit guides. However, they never provided me with any clear direction. The enemy KNOWS exactly what he is doing with the New Age deception. You get just enough insight or "light" to keep you searching, but you are never fulfilled. What changes everything? When you surrender to Christ, the Holy Spirit dwells within you, and suddenly the word of God spoke directly to my soul.

I had searched so long for a mentor, someone 'enlightened" enough to enlighten me. Now I had a built-in counselor, mentor, and guide, but I still needed to build a relationship with the Holy Spirit; I needed to learn what that sounded like. I had to learn to, and to be honest, I am still learning to trust and ask the Holy Spirit for guidance. Tools like Google or Chat GPT can be helpful, but we have to be careful about using them to replace what the Holy Spirit, Jesus and God can tell us.

Faith is a journey; it takes courage to turn away from the way of our world, from what society accepts as culturally appropriate. It is deafening right now that we must accept everything and everyone. We must be careful not to fall into the trap of being scared to speak our truth, especially if our truth is Jesus. The road to follow Jesus is absolutely beautiful and one that I will not get off of. But make no mistake that you will be ridiculed. Jesus told us,

"If the world hates you, keep in mind that it hated me first." (John 15:18).

This world crucified a perfect man; we must remember this. We live in a time when standing for the truth is perceived as hate, and love has been redefined to mean agreement with everything.

Society tells us that if you don't agree with me, you're judging me. Love means full acceptance of my choices; truth is relative, yours can't be above mine. As a follower of Christ, you are called,

> **"Do not conform to the pattern of this world, but be transformed by the renewing of your mind." (Romans 12:2).**

Jesus gave us the blueprint to heaven, we don't always understand it, and it isn't as restrictive as the enemy deceives people of. The enemy sells the idea of experiencing life and that nothing is good or bad, you are here to transcend" the matrix, to help elevate mass consciousness. It eliminates sin, the cross, the need of repentance or the blood of Jesus. The enemy sells you "freedom" from sin, but what you don't see are the chains of bondage he attaches in the spirit.

Satan doesn't want you to build a relationship with Jesus, the Holy Spirit or God, plain and simple, that is his plan. Because when you are connected and living fully in alignment with God, you build a protective spirit around you. Ephesians 6, "The more rooted you become in Christ, the more covered you are by his armor. With every step of faith, the enemy loses ground. I have grown my relationship with the Holy Trinity through a practice I have been using every morning. I invite the Holy Spirit into my presence and ask the Holy Spirit what I should know today. I have come to learn what the Holy Spirit sounds like through this discipline. The Holy Spirit has a grounded, relatable tone. The Spirit teaches me about concepts that enable me to align more deeply with God and Jesus. The spirit guides me when I ask questions and helps me discern things. I then invite Jesus into my presence. I also ask Jesus what he would like me to know. Jesus's presence feels like peace, like comfort, like complete love.

He is so kind and often teaches me about the law of God and the courts of heaven. He talks to me often about people and how they should be treated. Jesus saw people as they were before they were born; he saw them in their pure form, and he knew their true identity through Christ. We don't remember people by their words or actions, but by how they made us feel. Jesus is the purest example of this; to be seen the way Jesus sees us is the most beautiful, freeing gift we can receive. We see people and judge them by their outward appearance, we judge them by past interactions we had with them, but we never see them in their purest form before the world took its toll on them. We are incapable of loving like Jesus, but we can learn to treat people more like he did. He treated people with compassion, with grace, with humility, and most importantly, he didn't see their sin; he saw their soul. Jesus, teach this reader to see people through your eyes. Help this reader love without limits, speak truth with kindness, and serve without seeking anything in return. Let this reader's life be a reflection of You.

John 13:35, "By this everyone will know that you are my disciples, if you love one another."

Now Father God, he already knows what I need before I do, so I ask Father what do I need, it was softer in the beginning. Just as with learning anything, you build up your knowledge as you progress; building your relationship with the Holy Trinity is no different. As my relationship with God has progressed and I am learning to trust him as my father, his authority has come across stronger. Recently, he has convicted me of sharing my story in a way that isn't watered down, or that doesn't worry about the tone I am conveying. He is convincing me of why I am sharing. If I am not sharing for the sole purpose of helping others find Jesus, then I don't. He convicted me of not seeing all of my provisions coming from him. I was caught in the way of the world, thinking I just needed a little more. Yet God was clearly telling me I had enough; I was mismanaging what I had. God is Jehovah-Jireh, the Lord who provides (Genesis 22:14). He not only provides for us in financial abundance, but also for every need, including strength, peace, direction, and healing. God, this reader trusts you as their source and their sustainer. This reader releases their worry and receives their provision today, not just for their needs, but for the calling you've placed on their life.

We often become so caught up in letting go of what God is convicting us to release. We, in our humanness, struggle to see the direction, and we think we know a better way. When you obey what God directs you to do, He never takes something away without replacing it. What he replaces it with is always in alignment with what is best for you. We cause ourselves a lot of unnecessary suffering by being caught up in our fear of losing something. He is not a God of lack; he is a God of restoration, redemption, and divine exchange. God convicted me of residue lingering from the past. The Holy Spirit told me it was from the New Age that I needed to talk to my children, and it was time to open up completely about my faith journey. God also conveyed that I needed to unpublish the books I had written and the web pages associated with them that still had New Age residue on them.

At this point, I am beginning to understand that something even greater is going to replace the things I created. But that isn't my focus anymore, because as I am being stripped of beliefs, patterns, and materialistic creations, I am strengthening my ability to connect with the Holy Trinity. And that is the best thing I could ever receive. I used to think, why would I only be rewarded for a life well lived after I die? It sounded crazy to me that God would send his beloved children to hell for eternity, and quite honestly, it terrified me. He sent his only son to die for me, for all of us, so that we might live for eternity with him in the kingdom of heaven. But we have to stop being so selfish and foolish as to believe that salvation should be enough. I could never imagine giving my only child to come suffer, be murdered and resurrected to then have people curse my name because they wouldn't spend time learning my voice.

To have people unwilling to learn my word on how to live in alignment with my will, or to have people conform to the ways of the world instead of using discipline to overcome their flesh. We didn't and still don't deserve his salvation and grace, yet it is still there for us. He gave us all of this and is the source of all our goodness. Yet it still never seems enough for us because we have conformed to the world. Because we have let society shape our consumerism and warp our minds into believing we need more.

Mark 8:36, "What good is it for someone to gain the whole world, yet forfeit their soul?"

God is calling us back to him; he is asking us to redirect our need for things to the need for him. There comes a moment, often in the quiet, when the noise of the world fades and all that's left is Him, in the midst of heartbreak or surrender. And suddenly it clicks:

You don't need the approval.

You don't need the platform.

You don't need to be seen, applauded, or understood by anyone but the One who made you.

You don't even need all the answers.

You just need God.

You were never meant to be on your own, to carry the burden of life, the pressure you have been carrying? Lay it down before Jesus. The ache you can't name? The longing you can't fill? It is a holy hunger that God has placed in your heart, guiding you back home — to Him. I see you desperately clinging to self-perseveration. You can't let go, because you fear it will all crumble. And it might just crumble so that you can rebuild on the foundation of Jesus. So that you will never crumble again. There comes a time when God is all you have, and then he becomes all you have ever truly needed. Wherever you are, it is time to surrender, time to lay it all down, time to discover your identity through Christ, to build your relationship with the Holy Trinity, and to learn the blueprint — the blueprint to Heaven.

We went on The Journey, the journey I had through my faith. By the time this book is in your hands, it will be wholly transformed by the power of God.

It is time to move on to The Blueprint, where the Holy Spirit guides us on the way to live in alignment with God's will for your life, so that you can walk in purpose, experience true freedom, and become who you were created to be. We will conclude with 'The Way,' which is my morning conversations with the Holy Spirit, Jesus, and God. Solidified with scripture, they guide me to read. I lovingly called this The Way, because it is through this guidance that I found direction to my next destination. I hope you found yourself within my journey, and my biggest hope is that you found yourself closer to Jesus.

THE BLUEPRINT

Your relationship with God, Jesus and the Holy Spirit is intimately formed and is a deliberate act of faith and love. It takes time, trials, and tribulations. Just like with any relationship, you work together to build a bond. The blueprint gives you real, practical steps to help you do this. Everyone connects differently, as we are unique and learn differently. However, the goal remains the same: to build your relationships with the Holy Trinity and witness the transformation in your life. Our humanness will inevitably cause us some strife, and that is okay! God's grace is given to us so that we can make mistakes, and when we stumble, we are reminded that his love is greater. All of the steps are important and are designed to help you through all of the stages and transitions life brings. The most important steps to begin with are step one and step six. Learning your identity through God and building your relationships with the Holy Trinity will change everything.

Step One: Building the Foundation: We are made in the image of God.

When we grow in our awareness and understanding that our thoughts and words hold power, it allows us to be more careful and meaningful with them. This is the starting point to the blueprint, and if you build your blueprint on God, then it won't crumble. You begin by understanding what your identity is through

God, not the lies that you have learned.

> **Matthew 15:18-19, "But the things that come out of a person's mouth come from the heart, and these defile them. For out of the heart come evil thoughts, murder, adultery, sexual immorality, theft, false testimony, slander."**

It is important to connect with God's truth; it will shape your identity and change your life.

1. You were given dominion; God entrusted humanity with the responsibility to steward and govern the earth in alignment with his will.
2. Your words carry power

> **Proverbs 18:21, "The tongue has the power of life and death." Made in God's image, when we speak, our words create atmospheres and influence outcomes.**

3. Authority was restored through Christ, while sin distorted our authority; Jesus restored it.

Luke 10:19, "I have given you authority to trample on snakes and scorpions and to overcome all the power of the enemy; nothing will harm you."

4. Responsibility: You represent the kingdom of God; everywhere you go, you carry God's presence. This gives you the responsibility to reflect God's love and authority to others.

How to Walk in Your Authority:
- Get to know God's word; authority is exercised according to his truth, not through other people's opinions.
- Stay in alignment, authority flows from relationship; the closer you are to God, the stronger your spiritual authority.
- Use your voice by declaring God's promises over your life, family, and situations. (Promises of God are at the end of step one.)
- Resist the Enemy:

James 4:7, "Submit yourselves, then to God. Resist the devil, and he will flee from you."

Finding Your Identity Through God's Truth

This guide is designed to help you discover your true identity in Christ by seeking God's perspective, listening for His voice, and aligning with His Word.

Use these prompts to hear from Him, confirm with Scripture, and replace lies with His truth.

Steps to Finding Your Identity

- Quiet Your Heart - Find a peaceful space. Pray and invite the Holy Spirit to reveal God's truth about who you are.
- Prayer: Heavenly Father, In the name of Jesus, I come before you now. I invite your presence into this moment. I silence every voice that is not from you, every lie of the enemy, every distraction of my own mind, and every influence of the world. Holy Spirit, I welcome you to speak truth to my heart. Let your voice be the only one I hear. Open my ears to recognize your whisper, open my eyes to see your word come alive, and open my heart to fully receive what you are saying. Teach me who I am in your truth and show me how you see me. I surrender my thoughts, my emotions, and my will to you right now. In Jesus' name, Amen.
- Ask God - 'Father, how do You see me?' Write down what you sense, hear, or feel.
- Scripture Confirmation - Open your Bible and note the scripture that aligns with what you sensed.
- Ask - 'What is my true identity in Christ?' Record what comes to mind.
- Scripture Confirmation - Open your Bible again and write down the scripture that aligns.
- Ask - 'How has the enemy tried to corrupt or distort my identity?' Record what you feel God is showing you.
- Scripture Confirmation - Find a passage that speaks truth to counter that lie.

- Reflect - Write how these truths connect to your life and how you can walk in them daily.
- Prayer of Thanks - Close with gratitude, declaring your agreement with God's truth.

Ways God Speaks

-Through scripture that comes alive
-Through thoughts or impressions
-Through visions or mental images
-Through memories brought to mind
-Through the words of others
-Through peace or conviction in your spirit

Identity Discovery Worksheet

Father - How do You see me?
Scripture confirmation:
My true identity in Christ:
Scripture confirmation:
How has the enemy tried to corrupt my identity?
Scripture confirmation:
Reflection & Application:
Prayer of Thanks:

Promises of God

God's Presence

"The Lord himself goes before you and will be with you; he will never leave you nor forsake you." (Deuteronomy 31:8)

"And surely I am with you always, to the very end of the age."
(Matthew 28:20)

God's Provision

"And my God will meet all your needs according to the riches of his glory in Christ Jesus." (Philippians 4:19)

"The Lord is my shepherd, I lack nothing." (Psalm 23:1)

God's Protection

"The Lord will keep you from all harm—he will watch over your life." (Psalm 121:7–8)

"No weapon forged against you will prevail." (Isaiah 54:17)

God's Peace

"And the peace of God, which transcends all understanding, will guard your hearts and your minds in Christ Jesus." (Philippians 4:7)

"You will keep in perfect peace those whose minds are steadfast, because they trust in you." (Isaiah 26:3)

God's Guidance

"Trust in the Lord with all your heart and lean not on your own understanding; in all your ways submit to him, and he will make your paths straight." (Proverbs 3:5–6)

"Whether you turn to the right or to the left, your ears will hear a voice behind you, saying, 'This is the way; walk in it.'" (Isaiah 30:21)

God's Strength

"So do not fear, for I am with you; do not be dismayed, for I am your God. I will strengthen you and help you; I will uphold you with my righteous right hand. (Isaiah 41:10)

"But those who hope in the Lord will renew their strength. They will soar on wings like eagles." (Isaiah 40:31)

God's Salvation & Eternal Life

"For God so loved the world that he gave his one and only Son, that whoever believes in him shall not perish but have eternal life." (John 3:16)

"If we confess our sins, he is faithful and just and will forgive us our sins and purify us from all unrighteousness." (1 John 1:9)

Step Two: Patterns and Behaviors: Generational Iniquities

Now that we have built your foundation, uncovered your true identity through God, built an understanding of your authority through God's image, and grasped the power of your thoughts and words, it is now time to take a look at the patterns and behaviors at work in your life that have been passed down through generations. Many of us carry pain that didn't start with us; it is important to take a step back and look at how these are affecting us. The word of God teaches us that sin patterns can be passed down from generation to generation if they are not surrendered to God and broken through repentance. In Exodus 20:5, God says he ***"visits the iniquity of the fathers on the children to the third and fourth generation."***

This does not mean you are guilty of your ancestor's sins or agreements they made, but it does mean patterns can be inherited. These traits are not just learned; they can also be passed down biologically. Iniquity is not just one single sinful act; it is a bent of inclination toward a particular sin. It's when a way of living becomes so normalized in a family that it is repeated across multiple generations. Sin is the act; transgression is willfully crossing a known boundary, and iniquity is the deeply rooted pattern that fuels the sin over and over again. The iniquities that are passed down through generations are addictions, broken relationships, abuse, poverty mindset, anger and violence, control, and manipulation, rejecting God, occult practices, or worshipping other gods.

Breaking Generational Iniquities

This guide is designed to help you identify and break family patterns that are not from God. Generational iniquities are repeated behaviors, mindsets, and sins passed down through family lines. Through prayer, revelation, and the authority of Jesus Christ, these cycles can be broken so that blessings, not curses, are passed to future generations.

Steps to Breaking Generational Iniquities

- Quiet Your Heart - Find a peaceful space. Invite the Holy Spirit to reveal patterns in your family line.
- Ask God - 'Father, what generational iniquities exist in my family?' Write down what comes to mind.
- Scripture Confirmation - Open your Bible and note the scripture that aligns with what you sensed.
- Look Back - Think about your parents, grandparents, and great-grandparents. List behaviors or struggles that seem to repeat.
- Notice Patterns - Identify recurring themes such as addiction, broken relationships, poverty, anger, or spiritual apathy.
- Ask - 'Lord, how has the enemy used these patterns to keep my family bound?' Record what you feel God is showing you.
- Scripture Confirmation - Find verses that speak God's truth to counter those patterns.
- Declare Freedom - In Jesus' name, renounce and break agreement with these iniquities,
- declaring His authority over your life.

- Prayer of Thanks - Close with gratitude for the freedom God has given you and the new legacy He is building in your family.

Ways God Speaks

-Through scripture that comes alive
-Through thoughts or impressions
-Through visions or mental images
-Through memories brought to mind
-Through the words of others
-Through peace or conviction in your spirit

Prayer for Breaking Generational Iniquities

Heavenly Father, I come before You in the name of Jesus Christ, my Savior and Redeemer. I thank you You for the blood of Jesus that cleanses me from all sin and breaks every chain of the enemy. Lord, I acknowledge the patterns of iniquity in my family line, the sins, mindsets, and behaviors that have been passed down and have not honored You. I repent for the sins of my ancestors and for any way I have personally participated in or agreed with these patterns. In the authority of Jesus Christ, I break every agreement with these iniquities. I declare that the blood of Jesus breaks their power over me and my family. I speak life, blessing, and freedom over myself, my children, and future generations. Holy Spirit, fill every place where these patterns once had influence with Your truth, peace, and love. Father, I choose to walk in the identity and calling You have for me, leaving behind every curse and embracing the blessing of being Your child. In Jesus' name, Amen.

Generational Iniquities Worksheet

Holy Spirit - Reveal the generational iniquities in my family:
Scripture confirmation:
Family patterns I have noticed:
Recurring behaviors or struggles:
Lord, how has the enemy used these patterns?
Scripture confirmation:
My declarations to break these patterns:
Prayer of Thanks:

Step Three: Replacing Patterns with Healthy Behaviors

When you identify and take the root out of a pattern or belief, it is crucial to replace it with habits that honor yourself and God. Removing harmful patterns without replacing them leaves room for old habits to return. The things we repeat daily hold power over our lives; we have to be intentional with our time. Do not fall into the trap of believing that it is too late to change something or letting age become a factor. As long as you are breathing, it is a good time to grow and allow yourself the chance to feel true change.

> **Romans 12:2, "Do not conform to the pattern of this world, but be transformed by the renewing of your mind. Then you will be able to test and approve what God's will is, his good, pleasing, and perfect will."**

Replacing Patterns with Healthy Behaviors

Once harmful patterns are identified, it's important to replace them with habits that honor God. Simply removing a destructive pattern without replacing it leaves room for it to return. This guide will help you intentionally align your behaviors with God's Word.

Steps to Replacing Patterns with Healthy Behaviors

- Quiet Your Heart - Invite the Holy Spirit to guide you in this process.
- Identify - What harmful pattern or habit is God highlighting that needs to be replaced? Write it down.
- Scripture Confirmation - Ask God to show you a verse that addresses this pattern.
- Ask God - 'What healthy, God-honoring behavior can I replace this with?'
- Write the Replacement - Be specific about the new behavior you will adopt.
- Scripture Confirmation - Find a verse to anchor and reinforce the new behavior.
- Plan for Action - List practical steps you will take to practice the new behavior daily.
- Accountability - Identify someone who can encourage and check in with you.
- Prayer of Commitment - Commit the new habit to God, asking for His strength to walk it out.

Ways God Speaks

-Through scripture that comes alive

-Through thoughts or impressions

-Through visions or mental images

-Through memories brought to mind

-Through the words of others

-Through peace or conviction in your spirit

Prayer for Committing New Healthy Habits to God

Heavenly Father, I thank You for revealing the patterns in my life that do not honor You. Today, I choose to replace them with habits that reflect Your character and truth. Lord, I acknowledge that I cannot do this in my own strength, but through Christ, I can do all things. I commit this new habit to You and ask for the help of the Holy Spirit to guide me each day. When I am tempted to return to the old ways, remind me of the truth in Your Word and the calling You have placed on my life. I declare that my life, my words, and my actions will bring glory to You. Thank You for transforming me from the inside out and giving me the power to walk in victory. In Jesus' name, Amen.

Replacing Patterns Worksheet

Harmful pattern or habit to replace:
Scripture confirmation:
Healthy, God-honoring behavior to replace it with:
Scripture confirmation:
Practical steps for daily action:

Accountability partner(s):
Prayer of Commitment:
Lasting change:

Step Four: Understanding Your Body as a Temple

Your body is the temple of the Holy Spirit. Treating your body with respect

through healthy living allows you to feel good both physically, spiritually, and emotionally. When we think of our bodies as a gift from God, that we get to use in this life, it gives us a different lens at how we treat them.

Corinthians 6:19-20, "Do you not know that your bodies are temples of the Holy Spirit, who is in you, whom you have received from God? You are not your own; you were bought at a price. Therefore, honor God with your bodies."

Understanding Your Body as a Temple

Your body is a sacred dwelling place of the Holy Spirit. Scripture calls us to honor God with our bodies, which means caring for our physical health, avoiding what defiles us, and using our bodies to glorify Him. This guide will help you reflect on how to better steward your body as an act of worship.

Steps to Honoring Your Body as a Temple

- Quiet Your Heart - Invite the Holy Spirit to speak to you about how you care for your body.
- Ask God - 'Lord, how am I treating my body? Am I honoring You in how I care for it?'
- Scripture Confirmation - Find a verse that speaks to the value of your body as God's temple.
- Identify - What habits or actions may be dishonoring God in how you treat your body?
- Ask God - 'What changes do You want me to make to care for my body as Your temple?'
- List Healthy Habits - Write down the practical steps you will take to improve your care for your body.
- Scripture Confirmation - Anchor your commitment with a verse that inspires you to treat your body well.
- Plan for Accountability - Identify someone who can encourage you in your physical and spiritual health.
- Prayer of Dedication - Commit your body to the Lord for His purposes.

Ways God Speaks

-Through scripture that comes alive
-Through thoughts or impressions
-Through visions or mental images
-Through memories brought to mind
-Through the words of others
-Through peace or conviction in your spirit

Prayer for Honoring God with My Body

Heavenly Father, thank You for creating me in Your image and for making my body a temple for the Holy Spirit. Forgive me for the times I have not cared for it in a way that honors You. Today, I surrender my body to You completely, my health, my strength, my choices. Guide me in removing habits that harm me and replacing them with those that bring life. Remind me daily that caring for my body is not vanity but obedience and worship to You. Let everything I eat, drink, say, and do glorify Your name. In Jesus' name, Amen.

Body as a Temple Worksheet

Lord, how am I treating my body?
Scripture confirmation:
Habits or actions that may dishonor God:
Changes God wants me to make:
Healthy habits to adopt:
Scripture confirmation:
Accountability partner(s):
Prayer of Dedication:

Step Five: Consumption

What you consume not only physically affects you, but also has a mental and spiritual impact. Social media has taken over much of our time. We consume so much through it; some can be good, a vast majority can be detrimental. It is extremely important to monitor what you are taking in. God often convicts us of how we are using our time; are we using it to grow closer to him? Or are we allowing ourselves to be distracted?

> Proverbs 4:23-25, "Above all else, guard your heart, for everything you do flows from it. Keep your mouth free of perversity; keep corrupt talk far from your lips. Let your eyes look straight ahead; fix your gaze directly before you."

Consumption: Social Media vs. The Bible

What we consume daily shapes our thoughts, beliefs, and actions. Social media can be a tool for connection and inspiration, but it can also fill our minds with distraction, comparison, and lies. God's Word transforms our hearts and renews our minds. This guide will help you evaluate your daily consumption and align it with God's truth.

Steps to Aligning Your Consumption with God's Word

- Quiet Your Heart - Invite the Holy Spirit to help you assess your daily media use.
- Track - Write down how much time you spend on social media, TV, and other media compared to time in God's Word.
- Ask God - 'Lord, is what I'm consuming drawing me closer to You or pulling me away?'
- Scripture Confirmation - Find verses about guarding your heart and mind.

- Replace - Identify areas where you can reduce media consumption and replace them with Scripture reading or worship.
- Plan - Create a daily or weekly rhythm for consuming more of God's Word than worldly content.
- Accountability - Share your plan with someone who will encourage and check in with you.
- Prayer of Commitment - Dedicate your mind and heart to God's truth.

Ways God Speaks

-Through scripture that comes alive
-Through thoughts or impressions
-Through visions or mental images
-Through memories brought to mind
-Through the words of others
-Through peace or conviction in your spirit

Prayer for Guarding My Heart and Mind

Heavenly Father, I thank You for giving me access to Your Word, which is truth and life. I confess that I have sometimes filled my mind with things that do not honor You. Today, I choose to set my mind on what is true, noble, right, pure, lovely, and admirable. Help me to discern what I consume daily and to replace harmful or empty content with Your truth. Give me the strength to turn away from distractions and the discipline to spend more time with You than with the noise of the world.

I dedicate my eyes, ears, and mind to You, Lord. May what I take in always draw me closer to You. In Jesus' name, Amen.

<u>Consumption Worksheet</u>

Holy Spirit - Show me the truth about my media consumption:
Time spent on social media/TV vs. in God's Word:
Is what I'm consuming drawing me closer to God?
Scripture confirmation:
Areas to reduce world media:
Ways to increase time in God's Word:
Daily/weekly plan:
Accountability partner(s):
Prayer of Commitment:

Step Six: Letting Go and Building Your Relationship with the Holy Spirit, Jesus, and God

This is quite easily the most crucial step in the blueprint. It allows you to find your way, to gain insight, clarity, and build your relationship with the Holy Trinity. If you do anything in this blueprint, let it be this. These steps have transformed my life and the way I receive guidance and direction. When we learn the voice and tone of God, the Holy Spirit and Jesus, we can align our actions with them. It is the greatest gift we can give ourselves.

Jeremiah 29:12-13, "Then you will call on me and come and pray to me, and I will listen to you. You will seek me and find me when you seek me with all of your heart."

Letting Go and Building Your Relationship with the Holy Spirit

This guide is designed to help you surrender control, listen for God's voice, and deepen your relationship with the Holy Spirit each day.

Steps to Letting Go and Building Your Relationship with the Holy Spirit

- Quiet Your Heart - Find a peaceful space. Pray and invite the Holy Spirit to speak.
- Ask the Holy Spirit - 'Holy Spirit, what do I need to know today? What am I holding onto that I need to release?' Write down what you sense, hear, or feel.
- Scripture Confirmation - Open your Bible and note the scripture that aligns with what you sensed.
- Ask Jesus - 'Jesus, what do You want me to hear today?' Record what comes to mind.
- Scripture Confirmation - Again, open your Bible and write down the scripture that aligns.
- Scripture Confirmation - Open your Bible and note the scripture that aligns with what you sensed.
- Ask Jesus - 'Jesus, what do You want me to hear today?' Record what comes to mind.
- Scripture Confirmation - Again, open your Bible and write down the scripture that aligns.

- Let the Father Lead - Trust that God knows what you need. Ask Father God, what do I need? Open to a page and note the verse or passage that stands out.
- Reflect - Write how these verses connect to your life and the encouragement or correction they bring.
- Prayer of Surrender - Close with gratitude, committing your life to God's leading.

Ways God Speaks

-Through scripture that comes alive
-Through thoughts or impressions
-Through visions or mental images
-Through memories brought to mind
-Through the words of others
-Through peace or conviction in your spirit

Prayer of Surrender to the Holy Spirit

Holy Spirit, I thank You for being my Comforter, Teacher, and Guide. I confess that I have tried to control things instead of trusting You. Today, I choose to release everything I have been holding onto: my fears, my plans, my worries, and my need to be in control. I invite You to lead every part of my life. Teach me to hear Your voice clearly and to obey quickly. Fill me with Your peace and power so I can walk in alignment with God's will. I surrender my mind, my heart, and my steps to You. May my life be a reflection of Your love and truth. In Jesus' name, Amen.

Letting Go and Building Relationship Worksheet

Holy Spirit - What I sense:

Scripture confirmation:

Jesus - What I hear:

Scripture confirmation:

Father - Passage led to:

Reflection & Application:

Prayer of Surrender:

Step Seven: Overcoming Weakness and Attacks from the enemy

I wish that I could say that once you started growing in your faith, that everything would be easy and that the enemy would vanish, never to return again. The kingdom of darkness has limited resources, but if you are meant to serve a great purpose, that will not go unnoticed. This will open you up to attacks; the enemy will pinpoint weaknesses and strategically attack you. This doesn't mean you are defenseless; in fact, it is the opposite, as you have grown in your faith, built your relationship with God, and understand your authority. Be careful when you are being pulled into old habits or thought patterns; use discernment to understand where they are coming from.

> Ephesians 6:10-11, "Finally, be strong in the Lord and in his mighty power. Put on the full armor of God, so that you can take your stand against the devil's schemes."

James 4:7 - 'Submit yourselves, then, to God. Resist the devil, and he will flee from you.'

2 Corinthians 12:9-10 - 'My grace is sufficient for you, for my power is made perfect in weakness.'

1 Peter 5:8-9 - 'Be alert and of sober mind. Your enemy, the devil, prowls around like a roaring lion looking for someone to devour. Resist him, standing firm in the faith.'

Overcoming Weakness and Attacks from the Enemy

As you grow in your faith, the enemy often seeks to attack areas where you are still weak or vulnerable. God has given you spiritual authority, armor, and His Word as your defense. This guide will help you identify weaknesses, invite God's strength, and respond with biblical truth.

Steps to Overcoming Weakness and Attacks

- Pray for Discernment - Ask the Holy Spirit to reveal where the enemy may be attacking or tempting you.
- Identify Weaknesses - Write down areas where you struggle or feel spiritually vulnerable.
- Find Scripture Weapons - Search the Bible for verses that address each weakness.
- Pray for Strength - Ask God to fill those areas with His power and truth.
- Put on the Armor of God - Daily declare and apply Ephesians 6:10-18 over your life.

- Seek Accountability - Share your struggles with a trusted believer who can pray and walk with you.
- Stay Alert - Recognize triggers and spiritual patterns the enemy uses against you.

Prayer for Overcoming Weakness and Attacks

Lord God, I thank You that You are my refuge and strength, my ever-present help in trouble. I submit myself fully to You and resist the devil in the name of Jesus. I put on the full armor of God today - the belt of truth, the breastplate of righteousness, the shoes of peace, the shield of faith, the helmet of salvation, and the sword of the Spirit, which is the Word of God. Where I am weak, be my strength. Where I am tempted, be my escape. Where I am attacked, be my

defender. I declare that no weapon formed against me shall prosper, and every tongue that rises against me in judgment shall be condemned. Thank You for the victory I have in Christ. In Jesus' name, Amen.

Overcoming Weakness and Attacks Worksheet

Holy Spirit - Reveal where I am being attacked:
Areas of weakness I recognize:
Scriptures to speak against each attack:
Prayer for strength:
Daily declaration of the Armor of God:
Accountability partner(s):
Ways I will stay alert:

Step Eight: Asking for Guidance Through Transitions and Letting Go of People and Things That No Longer Serve You.

As we progress through our journey and follow God's path, there will be times when people we have built relationships with end up leaving. If you try to hold onto what God is asking you to let go of, it will delay your transition, or your interactions with them may cause frustrations, and just don't align with the path God is taking you down. I like to use the analogy of the proverbial meat grinder of life. This is when you are going through extremely difficult periods of your life. Quite literally, it feels like you are in a meat grinder; the grip is so strong, and it hurts to just get through your day. When you finally come out of the grinder, you are not the same; there are parts of you that have broken off, parts of you rearranged. This is meant for our growth; we often try to bring parts of us that God has been asking us to let go of. At some point, if we don't do it willingly, we are forced to. It can be so hard in the moment to understand why it is happening, but after you get out slowly, it starts to make sense. We can move forward carrying the past, and if you try, it becomes too heavy to carry.

Proverbs 3:5–6 – **"Trust in the Lord with all your heart and lean not on your own understanding; in all your ways submit to him, and he will make your paths straight."** Ecclesiastes 3:1 – **"There is a time for everything, and a season for every activity under the heavens."**

Isaiah 43:18–19 – "Forget the former things; do not dwell on the past. See, I am doing a new thing!"

Philippians 3:13–14 – "Forgetting what is behind and straining toward what is ahead, I press on toward the goal to win the prize…"

<u>Steps to Seeking Guidance and Letting Go</u>

- Pray for Clarity – Ask the Holy Spirit to reveal what is meant to stay in your life and what needs to be released.
- Examine Attachments – Identify people, habits, or possessions that may be holding you back from God's purpose.
- Surrender Control – Give God permission to remove what no longer serves His will.
- Seek Godly Counsel – Talk with mature believers who can give a biblical perspective.
- Replace with God's Truth – Fill the space with prayer, Scripture, and healthy, God-honoring relationships.
- Trust God's Timing – Remember that release is part of His preparation for the next season.
- Celebrate the New – Thank God in advance for the blessings to come.

Prayer for Guidance Through Transitions

Lord God,

I trust You with every season of my life. Where I have been holding on to what You are asking me to release, give me the courage to let go. Remove every person, habit, or possession that no longer serves Your will for me. Help me to see the beauty in Your plan, even when it feels uncomfortable. Fill the empty spaces with Your peace, Your truth, and Your presence. I choose to walk forward spaces with Your peace, Your truth, and Your presence. I choose to walk forward in faith, knowing You are making all things new.

In Jesus' name, Amen.

Guidance and Letting Go Worksheet

- Holy Spirit – Reveal what I need to release:
- People, habits, or possessions to let go of:
- Scriptures to meditate on during this transition:
- Prayer for strength to release:
- Steps I will take to replace old patterns with God-honoring ones:
- Godly counsel I will seek:
- Ways I will celebrate the new season:

Step Nine: Spiritual Warfare Prayers

Spiritual warfare is an ongoing battle between God's kingdom and the forces of darkness. As believers, we are called to stand firm in the authority that Christ has given us, resisting the enemy's attempts to overtake us. Take peace in the fact that God is far greater than Satan, but make no mistake about Satan's power. You won't outsmart Satan, but you can stand strong in your covenant with God.

Ephesians 6:12 - "For our struggle is not against flesh and blood, but against the rulers, against the authorities, against the powers of this dark world and against the spiritual forces of evil in the heavenly realms."

Corinthians 10:4-5 - "The weapons we fight with are not the weapons of the world. On the contrary, they have divine power to demolish strongholds."

James 4:7 - "Submit yourselves, then, to God. Resist the devil, and he will flee from you."

Luke 10:19 - "I have given you authority to trample snakes and scorpions and to overcome all the power of the enemy; nothing will harm you."

Steps

- Acknowledge the Battle - Recognize that the fight is spiritual, not physical.
- Put on the Armor of God - Daily declare and apply each piece from Ephesians 6:10-18.
- Use the Word as a Weapon - Speak Scripture to counter the enemy's lies.
- Pray with Authority - Bind the works of the enemy and loose God's truth and protection.
- Cover Others in Prayer - Intercede for family, friends, and fellow believers.
- Renounce and Break Agreements - Reject any foothold the enemy has through sin or past agreements.
- Praise and Worship - Shift the atmosphere by glorifying God.

Prayer

Heavenly Father, I thank You for the authority You have given me in Christ Jesus. I put on the full armor of God and stand firm against every scheme of the enemy. I declare that no weapon formed against me shall prosper. I bind every spirit of fear, confusion, and discouragement, and I loose Your peace, clarity, and joy over my life. Fill me with boldness to speak Your Word and the wisdom to recognize the enemy's tactics. I plead the blood of Jesus over myself, my spouse, my children, my house, my cars, my bank account, and everything under my stewardship. In Jesus' name, I claim victory through the blood of the Lamb. In Jesus' name, Amen.

Worksheet

-Areas where I sense spiritual attack:
-Scriptures I will use as weapons:
-Prayers I will pray daily:
-People I will cover in prayer:
-Agreements or sins I need to renounce:
-Ways I will incorporate praise and worship into my warfare:

Step Ten: Community

Can we do this alone? That is a great question. Jesus had a party of twelve. Being able to build your faith and have support from others doing the same is essential. Fellowship with other believers strengthens our faith, provides encouragement in trials, and allows us to serve and be served in love. It helps to keep us accountable and to hear from God through others. Because God often uses others to convey a message that you may need to hear.

Hebrews 10:24-25 - **"And let us consider how we may spur one another on toward love and good deeds, not giving up meeting together, as some are in the habit of doing, but encouraging one another, and all the more as you see the Day approaching."**

Ecclesiastes 4:9-10 - **"Two are better than one, because they have a good return for their labor: If either of them falls down, one can help the other up. But pity anyone who falls and has no one to help them up."**

Steps

- Seek a Christ-Centered Community - Connect with a local church, small group, or Bible study.
- Be an Active Participant - Engage in worship, prayer, and fellowship regularly.
- Serve Others - Use your gifts to help and encourage fellow believers.
- Be Vulnerable - Share your struggles and victories to foster deeper connections.
- Encourage and Pray for Others - Strengthen your community through love and intercession.
- Stay Accountable - Allow trusted believers to speak truth into your life.
- Invite Others - Share the gospel and welcome new believers into the family of faith.

Prayer

Lord God, Thank You for the gift of community. Surround me with people who will strengthen my faith, speak truth into my life, and encourage me in Your ways. Help me to be a source of love, encouragement, and support to others. Show me how to use my gifts to serve my community and glorify You. Unite us in Your Spirit so that we may reflect the love of Christ to the world. In Jesus' name, Amen.

Worksheet

-Communities I am currently a part of:
-Ways I can participate more fully:
-Gifts or skills I can offer to serve others:
-People I will intentionally encourage and pray for:
-Areas where I need accountability:
-Steps I will take to invite others into community:

Connect with Me

YouTube: https://www.youtube.com/@amieburnis6745

Instagram: https://www.instagram.com/soulfed_blueprint/profilecard/igsh=cWZ2Ymh5YzdheTdy

Facebook Group: https://www.facebook.com/share/1Ayio4DVhj/?mibextid=wwXIfr

THE WAY

*I*n my journey of faith, I searched for so long that I tried anything that came my way. Praying that I would find the solution to my circumstance,

which I thought needed to be changed. I desperately wanted to find "the truth," and I was seeking something I couldn't quite put my finger on. I thought I could affirm my way out of it; vision cast my way out of it or think my way through it. None of that held any lasting power; it has only changed as I hold tight to the path God has laid out for me. Jesus told us that No one comes to the Father except through me (John 14:6). I didn't always understand what that meant before; I didn't know that Jesus was the way.

The Holy Spirit revealed that my connection to God depends on my relationship with his son. When I fully committed to accepting Jesus as my savior, was when my veil fell. No longer did I spend hours searching for the truth, no more crystals, affirmations, meditations, or mediums.

Just surrendering to Jesus, and fully knowing he truly is the way, the truth, and the life. My love and devotion to Jesus is the most important thing to me, not only because he is our Lord and Savior, but because he saved my life. He gave purpose to my pain and restored parts of my heart that I never thought would heal. I had spent well over a decade trying to repair it myself, and Jesus just swept in and made me new. The best part is he took my guilt and shame and turned them into purpose.

For so long, I wanted to serve others, so that they might see their worthiness. When I became a believer, I realized it had absolutely nothing to do with me and everything to do with guiding them to build a relationship with Jesus. Sometimes I felt helpless while trying to guide others, but now I know everything is possible with Jesus. It was through my growth that I came to understand the only way to fully commit my life to God is to build a relationship with Jesus, God, and the Holy Spirit. I knew it would take consistency, repetition, and time. It would take trust, love, and faith. To accomplish this, I set up a morning routine I called The Way, because it truly is my way through life, as the holy trinity has revealed so much to me through this practice. I will show you the practice, an example and share some insights I have gleaned through it.

Morning Routine: Deepening Your Relationship with the Father, Son & Holy Spirit

This morning routine is designed to help you grow in intimacy with the Father, Jesus, and the Holy Spirit. It blends prayer, listening, scripture, and journaling so you can recognize how God speaks to you and live guided by His presence each day.

- Quiet Your Heart – Find a peaceful space. Pray and invite the Holy Spirit to speak.
- Ask the Holy Spirit – 'Holy Spirit, what do I need to know today?' Write down what you sense, hear, or feel.
- Scripture Confirmation – Open your Bible and note the scripture that aligns with what you sense. Let the Holy Spirit guide you to the page.
- Ask Jesus – 'Jesus, what do You want me to hear today?' Write down what comes to mind.
- Scripture Confirmation – Again, open your Bible and write down the scripture that aligns. Allow Jesus to guide you to the page.
- Let the Father Lead – Trust that God knows what you need. Allow God to lead you to whatever it is; maybe it is conviction. Never shy away from this.

God leads you exactly where you need to go, for your highest good. To let go of what is holding you back. Open to a page directed by God and note the verse or passage that stands out.

- Reflect – Write how these verses connect to your life and the encouragement or correction they bring.
- Prayer of Thanks – Close with gratitude, committing your day to God.

Ways God Speaks:

- Through scripture that comes alive
- Through thoughts or impressions
- Through visions or mental images
- Through memories brought to mind
- Through the words of others
- Through peace or conviction in your spirit

The following is an example of a morning spent with the Holy Trinity:

Holy Spirit's response to me: peace is living in alignment with God, knowing even through troubled waters, he is holding you. He never fails you. Jesus knew this perfectly. God didn't make you to be ordinary. He made you extra extraordinary. When you're calling is great, your skills and strength must be strong. The scripture I felt called to open to: Romans 5:5," therefore, since we have been justified, that is, acquitted of sin, declared blameless before God by faith, let us grasp the fact that we have peace with God and the joy of reconciliation with him through our Lord Jesus Christ, the Messiah, the anointed. Through him, we also have access by faith into this remarkable state of grace, in which we firmly and securely stand. Let us rejoice in our hope and the confident assurance of experiencing and enjoying the glory of our great God, the manifestation of his excellence and power. And not only this, but with joy let us exalt in our suffering, and rejoice in our hardships, knowing that hardship (distress, pressure, trouble) produces patient endurance; and endurance, proven character (spiritual maturity); and proven character, hope, and confident assurance of eternal salvation. Such hope in God's promises never disappoints us, because God's love has been abundantly poured out within our hearts through the Holy Spirit, who was given to us. This brought tears to my eyes; the love and strength I felt were so valuable.

Jesus gave me the following answer: The Father loves you so deeply that He is unfailing; the reward of heaven is far greater than anything we will go through on earth. The flesh isn't here for a long time, but a good time(honestly, I think Jesus has a great sense of humor). The flesh seeks to defile and destroy, but the flesh is limited. The soul and spirit are eternal. Psalm 121: my help comes from the Lord, who made heaven and earth. He will not allow your foot to slip; the Lord is your keeper, the Lord is your shade on your right hand. The sun will not strike you by day, nor the moon by night; the Lord will protect you from all evil. He will keep your life. The Lord will guard your going out and your coming in from this time forth and forever. Again, the scripture completed his words to me. Please know, sometimes the scripture I find doesn't always make sense in relation to what I received in answer from the Holy Trinity.

Father God's guidance to me: obedience provides the path to me. I don't make it harder for you, but without learning a skill, how will you grow? The hardest trials come to those who have great gifts. Each trial builds your armor. Scripture: Proverbs 9:8: Give instruction to a wise man, and he will become an even wiser teacher, righteous man, and he will increase his learning.

The fear of the Lord, that is, worshiping him and regarding him, is truly awesome. It is the beginning and the pre-eminent part of his wisdom, and the knowledge of the holy one is understanding, understanding and spiritual insight for by me, wisdom from God, your days will be multiplied, in your years of life will be increased. If you were wise, you were wise for yourself; if you scoff thoughtlessly, ridicule, and disdain, you alone will pay the penalty. The foolish woman is restless and noisy. she is naïve and easily misled and thoughtless, and knows nothing at all of eternal value. She sits at the doorway of her house on a seat by the high and conspicuous places of the city, calling to those who pass by, who are making their path straight, whoever is naïve or inexperienced. Let him turn in here, and to him who lacks understanding she says stolen, waters pleasures are sweet because they are forbidden, and bread eaten in secret is pleasant, but he does not

know that the spirit of the dead are there and that her guests are already in the depths of Sheol, another world, the place of the dead.

A wise son makes a father glad, but a foolish son is a grief to his mother. Treasures of weakness and ill-gotten gains do not profit, but righteousness and moral integrity in daily life rescues from death. The Lord will not allow the righteous to hunger; God will meet all his needs, but he will reject and cast away the craving of the wicked.

I have come to learn the tone, the direction and the guidance style of God, Jesus, and the Holy Spirit. The Holy Spirit truly feels like my counselor, my director and guidance. For a long time, I believed the answers were all within me. I thought that if I just believed enough and trusted myself enough, the answer would reveal itself. But the truth is, my own wisdom is limited, and my heart can be deceived. I now see it's not me within me; it is the Holy Spirit within me. Jesus promised in John 14:26 that the Holy Spirit would teach us all things and remind us of His truth. The spirit living inside me is my guide, my counselor, my source of wisdom, without self-reliance. The Holy Spirit comes to me with words of guidance and direction and gives me depth to concepts I am wrestling with.

The Holy Spirit is always there when I ask. The most important part of this is that I can always back up with what I receive with scripture, and oftentimes I will randomly open a page with a passage that is exactly what the Holy Spirit revealed. That is not happenstance, that is God. When I call on Jesus, I often get visuals as he explains God's word and his works. He brings such peace and love; it doesn't feel like I am being reprimanded and feels so pure. You can feel his love for us and his love for the father. Sometimes it can be overwhelming to think about the sacrifice Jesus made for us, but I honestly think that is why it is so important to understand his teachings. To model his love for others, we will never be able to love like he did. But we can ask for his eyes to see others the way he was able to, we can ask for his heart to love others the way he did.

It can be easy at the beginning of your walk with Jesus to get "stuck" in the trap of focusing on others' sins. But Jesus didn't do that; he knew what they did and loved them through it. It isn't our job to keep track of others' sins. We can see the corruption Satan has created on Earth, and it is so easily seen in the division of people in political parties. He created this divide so that we wouldn't come together as God intends us to. Instead of seeing others' sins and thinking that if you still love the person, you aren't valuing your beliefs, maybe see that the enemy has created barriers so that the person hasn't been able to connect fully with God. That allows you to just see them as human and helps to take away the judgement. Remember, Jesus died for us and our sins; let God handle the rest.

God our Father, he is definitely awe-inspiring. Sometimes, I want to understand him better, which is quite the undertaking. Instead, I realize building my relationship with him will deepen my capacity to surrender. God has the authority figure feeling, but it doesn't feel like he corrects me out of anger or punishment; it feels like he is a parent guiding me to align with his will for my life. Surrendering to God's will requires conviction, which is taking a deeper look into what God calls you to. Sometimes the conviction hurts a bit, but it is ALWAYS in your best interest. He knows what you need and what you shouldn't take with you. It actually is a gift to let go of what is holding you back. Picture us traversing through life, but we are in the pitch black. We start to walk alone with our finite understanding. God offers us a light so we can see the path. But because we can't see the entire path lit up before us, we sometimes doubt his direction.

We then start to wander; we start to see that he is taking us to the base of a mountain. So, in a panic, we decided to turn because we didn't want to climb, but what we didn't see was the cliff he was redirecting us from. We also didn't see the view from the mountain we would climb, or the character it would build as we worked through the challenge.

That is why God's guidance is so necessary, and surrendering to his will is essential. It isn't out of punishment or a want to control, it is out of pure love for us. Just as hard as it is to watch your children learn to walk, and the number of times they fall or bump into something, you have to let them struggle through it. Because you know you cannot learn it for them, and they get to build a new skill. God has to do the same for us, watching us fumble our way through things, and make no mistake, it hurts him to see us hurt, but he steps into our hurt with us. Through Jesus, he carried our sorrows (Isaiah 53:4). You have no idea how much this routine will change your life. Some days you will struggle to connect, do it anyway. Some days are harder than others, because our thoughts take us away from God and into worry. As long as you continue to surrender to God and this practice, you will be able to face whatever challenges come your way.

I will never promise that your walk with God takes away all of the pain, or that you won't have moments of anger at God's plan. We will never fully be able to understand why things happen, and we must remember that the enemy is hard at work to corrupt and destroy. But we also need to put our trust in God's unwavering love for us.

Surrendering to God means making him the most important part of your work. It means making him bigger and yourself smaller. The enemy has strategies that you must be aware of. Satan knows the ego is fragile; he loves to feed you lies like your worth depends on others noticing you. Comparison is a terrible thing that pulls us out of humility and peace and stirs up conflict. Real strength is in surrender, letting God's voice be louder than yours. Ask Jesus to help quiet your ego, ask to think like Jesus, every single day. The enemy and ego try to convince us that our voice must dominate. God calls us to make room for his voice; when we decrease, he increases (John 3:30).

Being grounded in who God says you are is imperative to your growth. The world is so loud and can pull you into lies that are not true. There are moments when you feel the lies quiet and you can literally feel Jesus' presence, and then there are moments when you can feel spiritual battles taking place. During those moments, no matter how hard they are, do not allow your thoughts to take control. The times when you are struggling, remember God's grace, the enemy aims to wear you out, mentally, physically and spiritually. God doesn't want you to win these fights alone. Remember, we fight from victory, not for victory. Jesus already won on the cross; his spirit strengthens us to endure when our own willpower is gone. What does grace look like in battle? Rest when you want to strive, instead of scrambling to fix it, trust God's timing. Pray instead of reacting, grace slows us down so we respond in the spirit, not the flesh. Forgive even in attack, just as Christ forgave on the cross. Lord, remind us in this fight that it is not my power but yours that sustains me. Cover me with your grace when I feel weak, when ego pushes me to defend myself, or when the enemy whispers lies. Help me stand firm, clothed in your armor, and resting in the truth that victory is already yours. Amen.

Remembering God's Grace During Spiritual Battles

Step 1: Pause and Acknowledge the Battle

Don't ignore it or let ego rush you into reacting. Simply stop and name what's happening.

"Be alert and of sober mind. Your enemy the devil prowls around like a roaring lion looking for someone to devour." (1 Peter 5:8)

Practice: Take one deep breath, whisper: 'Lord, I know this is a battle, and I give it to You.'

Step 2: Remember God's Grace Covers You

When guilt, shame, or fear rise up, remind yourself that His grace is already sufficient.

"My grace is sufficient for you, for my power is made perfect in weakness." (2 Corinthians 12:9)

Practice: Say: 'Your grace is enough for me, even right now.'

Step 3: Put On Your Armor

You don't need to invent your own strength — God has already provided spiritual armor.

"Put on the full armor of God, so that you can take your stand against the devil's schemes." (Ephesians 6:11)

Practice: Pray through the armor (helmet of salvation, breastplate of righteousness, shield of faith, sword of the Spirit, belt of truth, feet fitted with readiness).

Step 4: Resist Ego's Urge to Be Heard

The enemy often works through pride and defensiveness. Grace calls you to stillness and trust.

"The Lord will fight for you; you need only to be still." (Exodus 14:14)

Practice: When you want to defend yourself, pray instead: 'Lord, You for me.'

Step 5: Stand in Grace, Not Fear

The outcome doesn't depend on you — it depends on God's victory through Christ.

"No weapon formed against you shall prosper." (Isaiah 54:17)

"Thanks be to God! He gives us the victory through our Lord Jesus Christ." (1 Corinthians 15:57)

Practice: Declare out loud: 'I already have victory in Jesus.'

Step 6: Rest and Rejoice in God's Presence

After the storm, or even in the middle of it, let grace move you into peace.

"Be still, and know that I am God." (Psalm 46:10)

"The joy of the Lord is your strength." (Nehemiah 8:10)

Practice: Put on a worship song, journal what God is teaching you, or simply sit in silence and thank Him.

Summary

- Pause & acknowledge the battle.
- Remember His grace is enough.
- Put on God's armor.
- Resist ego's urge to be heard.
- Stand in grace, not fear.
- Rest & rejoice in His presence.

My prayer through this book is that it has inspired you to grow closer to God, to allow him to lead, to surrender to his will for you and to build your relationship with Jesus. I know how hard the battles are that you wage every day in your head, because I, too, fight them. I am reminded that in moments when I feel the need for significance, nothing else matters but giving glory to God. Through all the pain, the fear and doubt, I know God has me. It has been such a journey through all of the growth, lessons and challenges. From church to New Age, to following Jesus, each one brought a piece of life's puzzle that brought me to this exact moment. Life is a true gift; we often take for granted day to day how precious it is because we get caught up in the mundane routine we lead. But if we remind ourselves that in each moment we can stop and connect with God, it is our true-life line.

Heavenly Father, I thank you for this reader. I ask that you remind them of their true identity. I ask that Jesus reveal the lies the enemy has spoken into them, that he takes them and burns them at the foot of the cross. Lord, fill this reader with your love, and help them remember your sacrifice every day so that they might spend eternity with you.

Lord, please let them know that while our burdens are heavy, remind them that your yoke is easy and your burden is light. Lord, I ask that you reveal yourself to this reader, and that they surrender to your guidance. Father, I ask that this reader decrease and that you increase, and I ask this reader to humble themselves as you have said you will lift us up. Lord, you told us that no one comes to the Father except through you. Lord, be the connection for this reader so they might know God more intimately than ever before. I pray all of this in Jesus' name, Amen.

I see all of you, I truly love you, and I pray for your growth in faith. I pray you surrender to God, even through the pain and struggle. I pray that you know just how loved you are and how wanted you are. That you know that God made you for a specific purpose and with perfect love. I pray that a smile comes to your face when you sense Christ with you. I pray your eyes fill with tears when you think about Jesus thinking about you some 2,000 years in the future as he prepared for his death to save you. I love you, I see you, and I pray for your growth in relationships with God, Jesus and the Holy Spirit.

References

Holy Bible, Amplified Bible. (2015). The Lockman Foundation.

Holy Bible, New International Version. (2011). Zondervan. (Original work published 1978)

Liddell, H. G., & Scott, R. (1996). A Greek-English lexicon (9th ed.). Oxford University Press.

www.ingramcontent.com/pod-product-compliance
Lightning Source LLC
Chambersburg PA
CBHW060404080526
44583CB00012B/464